Género Fantasía

¿? **Pregunta esencial**
¿Qué se ve en el cielo?

El nuevo hogar de la familia Zorro

Daniel Haikin
ilustrado por Fian Arroyo

CAPÍTULO 1

Una casita de juguete

La familia Zorro quiere construir otro hogar. El nuevo hogar estará debajo de un árbol gigante. Jaime y Laura son muy pequeños para ayudar a Mamá y Papá Zorro.

—¿Por qué no hacen una casita de juguete? —pregunta Papá Zorro.

—Veamos quién hace la casa más grande —dice Jaime.

—No. Veamos quién hace la casa más resistente —dice Laura.

Jaime hace un hoyo en el suelo.

"Mi casa será muy grande",
piensa Jaime.

Laura clava palitos para hacer las paredes de su pequeña casa. Luego, los cubre con barro.

—Mi casa será muy fuerte —dice Laura.

—Le pondré un techo de caucho —dice Jaime.

—No podrás hacerlo hoy —dice Laura—. Mira, está empezando a oscurecer.

—Es verdad —dice Jaime.

CAPÍTULO 2

Alcanzar el sol

Mamá Zorro llama a los niños:

—¡Vengan! Ya son las seis. El sol ya se pone.

Jaime está enfurruñado. Tiene muchas ganas de terminar su casa.

—Mamá, ¿podemos pedirle a nuestro amigo sol que no se ponga tan rápido? —pregunta Laura.

—Está bien. Pero sean educados con él —dice Mamá Zorro—. Y no tarden mucho.

Detective del lenguaje ¿A quién se refiere el pronombre personal subrayado?

Laura y Jaime corren una carrera hasta el sol.

—¡Mira! —dice Laura—. ¡El sol ya se va!

—Exacto. ¡Corramos! —responde Jaime.

Los zorritos persiguen al sol. Caminan y saltan entre los arbustos, el pasto, las rocas.

Detective del lenguaje

La coma (,) indica que debes hacer una pausa breve al leer. Encuentra las comas en esta página y di qué separan.

—¡Amigo sol! —aúlla Jaime—. ¡Espera!

El gigante sol saluda a los niños:

—Hola, muchachitos. ¿Qué hacen acá?

—Hola, ¿nos harías un favor? ¿Te quedarías un rato más? —pregunta Laura—. Queremos seguir jugando.

—Y Papá y Mamá Zorro quieren seguir trabajando —agrega Jaime.

CAPÍTULO 3

Buenas noches

El sol se ofrece a quedarse un ratito.

—Vamos a ver qué hacen su mamá y su papá —les dice.

El sol y los zorritos van juntos al nuevo hogar de la familia Zorro. Mamá y Papá están contentos de recibir al sol. Laura y Jaime juegan más.

—¿Por qué no te quedas allí arriba todo el tiempo? —pregunta Jaime.

—No puedo —responde el sol y bosteza—. Estoy cansado. ¡Ya es hora de dormir! Hasta mañana, mis peludos amiguitos.

Los cuatro zorros se despiden del sol y se van a dormir a su nuevo hogar debajo del árbol.

Respuesta a la lectura

Volver a contar

Vuelve a contar *El nuevo hogar de la familia Zorro* con tus propias palabras.

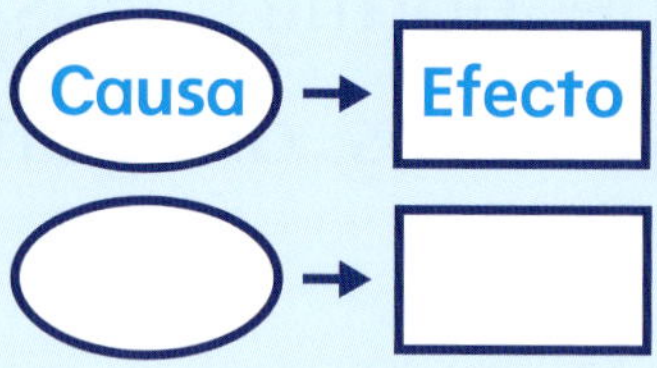

Evidencia en el texto

1. Mira la página 6. ¿Cuál es la causa de que el sol se ponga?
   Causa y efecto

2. ¿Por qué Jaime y Laura no quieren que el sol se ponga? Causa y efecto

3. ¿Cómo sabes que *El nuevo hogar de la familia Zorro* es un cuento de fantasía? Género

Género No ficción

Compara los textos

Lee más sobre el Sol.

Cuando la Tierra gira, se originan el día y la noche.

Amanecer y atardecer

Vemos que el Sol sale por el este. A la mañana, parece que sube cada vez más alto en el cielo. A la tarde, parece que se esconde poco a poco. Al final del día, desaparece por el oeste. ¿Cruza de un lado al otro del cielo? No. El Sol no se mueve. ¡La Tierra se mueve!

Mientras la Tierra gira, una mitad queda de cara al Sol. En esa mitad de la Tierra es de día. La otra mitad queda del lado opuesto al Sol. Allí es de noche.

(bkgd) Tetra Images RF/Getty Images, (t) Carlos Davila/Photographer's Choice RF/Getty Images, (bl) iconics/a.collectionRF/amana images/Getty Images, (br) Tom Stewart/Corbis/Getty Images

El amanecer y el atardecer son parecidos. En esos momentos, el cielo se ilumina con bellos colores. Pero también son diferentes. ¿Qué haces al amanecer? ¿Qué haces al atardecer?

Esta familia se sienta junto a una fogata al atardecer.

¿? Haz conexiones

Mira ambas selecciones. ¿Cómo está el cielo cuando el Sol se pone?

El texto y otros textos

Published in 2025 by The Rosen Publishing Group, Inc.
2544 Clinton Street, Buffalo, NY 14224

Editor: Ashley Brown
Designer: John Woolford

Cataloging-in-Publication Data

Names: Brewer, Paul.
Title: Warfare in the ancient world / Paul Brewer.
Description: New York: Rosen Publishing, 2025. | Series: Warfare through the centuries | Includes glossary, index, and bibliographic information
Identifiers: ISBN 9781499478556 (pbk) | ISBN 9781499478563 (library bound) | ISBN 9781499478570 (ebook)
Subjects: LCSH: History—Military—Ancient—juvenile literature | Military history, Ancient—juvenile literature | Military art and science—juvenile literature | Warfare—juvenile literature
Classification: LCC U29 .B74 2025 | DDC 355.0093--dc24

PICTURE SOURCES
Front Cover: Public Domain: Hunterian Museum and Art Gallery/Conelis Court. Interior: Alamy: Aclosund Historic 31, Granger Historical Picture Archive 50, The Picture Art Collection 28, 59; Library of Congress: Louvre Museum 19, 34, Tretyakov Gallery 70; Look and Learn: Rijksmuseum 35; Metropolitan Museum of Art: Fletcher Fund 69; Public Domain: 32, 74, American Numismatic Society 56, Museum of Antiquities 57, Britania 73, Cassell's Illustrated Universal History 30, Ulpiano Checa 72, Chinese Tomb Artist/Michael Sullivan's Art of China 77, Musee Dauphinois 44, Joh Steeple Davis 23, Diego Delso 68, Dorothea Gray 8, Mary Harrsch/British Museum on loan to Getty Villa 1, 15, Hunterian Museum and Art and Art Gallery 49, Hutchinston 38, Joachim Ibarra/scanned by Shlavozensky 54, Internet Archive Book Images/flickr 43, Kunstmuseum Basel 66, Austen Henry Layard 13 Jona Lendering/Livius.org 20, Lippisches Landesmuseum Detmold/www.iwi.org 60, Louvre Museum 61, Louvre Museum/ Jastrow 7, Naples National Archaeological Museum 40, National Musuems Scotland 16, New York Ward, Lock/The Illustrated History of the World 10, Peltast 24, RMN/Palace of Versailles 36, The Yorck Porject/Bibliotheque Nationale de France/gallica.bnf.fr 5, The Yorck Project/Museum of Fine Arts Budapest 52, Yale University Art Gallery 46; Shutterstock: Michael Rosskothen 21, Kevin Standage 62.

All other photography and artwork Brown Bear Books.

Some of the images in this book illustrate individuals who are models. The depictions do not imply actual situations or events.

Manufactured in the United States of America

CPSIA Compliance Information: Batch #CW25RYA. For further information, contact Rosen Publishing, New York, New York, at 1-800-237-9932.

CONTENTS

Introduction

Warfare has dominated human activity since the earliest times. This volume looks at wars from the dawn of recorded history to the collapse of the Roman Empire in the 5th century CE. At the beginning of this era conflicts were often between tribes and fought by men on foot armed with wooden or stone weapons. Wars were localized and short-lived.

As time passed, great empires were founded that maintained regular standing armies whose ranks were filled with trained soldiers armed with metal weapons. Wars became longer and were fought over much greater distances, although the movement of armies and their resupply remained difficult throughout the period. Battlefield tactics became refined and several generals, notably Alexander the Great and Hannibal, were truly outstanding leaders.

The Romans, who came to control the ancient world of the Mediterranean, were able to keep large armies in the field for months, unlike most of their enemies. Roman soldiers also displayed a professionalism that, after the fall of the Roman Empire, would not begin to be seen again until the late 15th century.

Some of Rome's success was because its enemies had to stop fighting to gather their harvests. The empire often had time to recover from any defeat or could pursue its enemies back to their homelands. Rome itself produced enough surplus food—and was rich enough to buy it from other sources during a famine—to keep its armies fighting all year if needed.

The Romans were also great military engineers and were able to build fortifications to protect their empire's frontiers. They were also able to create temporary forts, bridges, and roads, all of which gave them a considerable edge over their opponents. The importance of the different types of soldiers varied throughout the period. For a brief period horse-drawn chariots were often used in Egypt and China, but were replaced by foot soldiers. The trained, spear-armed infantry of the Greek city-states, the massed phalanx pike-blocks used to devastating effect by Alexander, and the sword-armed Roman legionaries time and again defeated enemy cavalry and less well-trained infantry.

By the time of the fall of the Roman Empire, the cavalryman had pretty much replaced the foot soldier as the key battlefield weapon. Cavalrymen moved more quickly than foot soldiers and could deliver powerful charges that often swept enemy infantry from the battlefield. Infantry now often just supported the more-powerful cavalrymen on the battlefield.

Few rulers after the fall of the Roman Empire had the resources to maintain a large army. Most relied on a core of semiprofessional soldiers, mainly nobles and their bodyguards. Many of the military techniques developed by the Romans were lost and not rediscovered until much later. For a time after the end of Rome, warfare was what it had been in the past—a fight between poorly-trained soldiers commanded by warrior-leaders.

The Beginnings of Warfare

Two of the earliest known cities date from about 7000 BCE. These are Jericho and Catal Huyuk in the Middle East. Both cities had walls to protect them from attack. This shows that warfare is as old as urban civilization itself. It was certainly part of the human experience long before written history. Historians have long debated whether war came about because humans are naturally violent. Whatever the root cause, war in the earliest times slowly became more complex, while weapons technology improved.

This illustration, *The Fall of Jericho* by Jean Fouquet (c. 1420-1477/81), shows priests blowing their trumpets as the crowd cheers and the walls of Jericho crumble.

Weapons fall into two categories—those that are thrown or shot and those used at close range. The bow and the sling are examples of the first category, the club and the knife of the second. The spear features in both. Lighter, shorter spears can be thrown in the way that some track-and-field athletes hurl the javelin. Longer, heavier ones, often wielded in both hands, can be used to stab at the enemy, giving the advantage of a longer reach over enemies armed with a shorter knife, sword, or club.

When Did Warfare Begin?

There is no hard evidence of how or when warfare began. Historians guess that bands of humans first fought over land or watering places, or to acquire food. The only Stone Age cultures about which historians know a great deal are the highly developed Aztec and Mayan ones in Latin America. Their goal in battle was to capture an enemy, not kill him. The winning side would then demand tribute in the form of produce or goods.

Because of this the Aztecs and Mayans used weapons that were intended to disable instead of to kill. A dead man could not be sacrificed to the Aztec or Mayan gods. The importance placed on capture is highlighted by the art of the Mayans, which always shows a warrior with a captive.

Every Aztec boy trained to be a warrior but not all gained a permanent place in the warrior house of their clan. A warrior gained such honors only when he had captured his fourth enemy soldier on the field of battle. However, the price of failure was harsh. A soldier had only two or three campaigning seasons in which to capture a prisoner. If he failed to do so in that time, he lost his right to be a warrior. A successful soldier was in the same way expected to keep to this standard of conduct on the battlefield. The punishment for failure was loss of his warrior status for the next one or two seasons of campaigning and battle.

The Aztec army drew its commanders from among those who had taken five or more enemy captives. The questions they faced were the same ones that have confronted any general at any level of civilization. These fall into two categories, those of strategy and those of tactics.

Strategy and Tactics

The overall plan to fight a war falls under the heading of strategy. At the start of a military campaign a commander must ask himself several questions. Where shall I gather my army? In which direction shall we march? Should the army's soldiers march together or in separate units? Where will the enemy be? How many scouts should I send out and where?

Once the location of the enemy is known, the commander turns to questions of tactics—deciding how the battle will be fought. How shall I deploy my forces? Is it a good idea to try to ambush the enemy? Should I attack by day or night? Should my main attack be directed toward one of my enemy's flanks or at his center? If we win how far should I pursue? How can I protect my own line of retreat if we lose?

However, warfare is not a pure science, and answering the questions of strategy and tactics has never been the whole story. Luck has often played its part in both battles and campaigns, as have surprise and deception. By using surprise and deception,

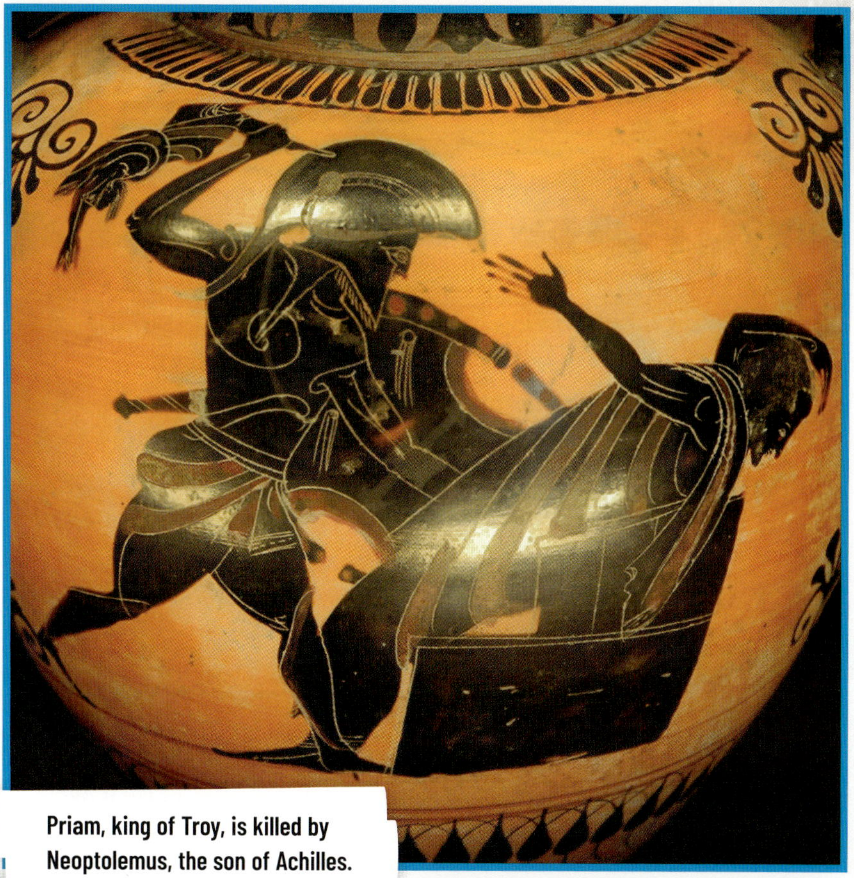

Priam, king of Troy, is killed by Neoptolemus, the son of Achilles. The capture of the city of Troy by the Greeks demonstrated the importance of deception in war from earliest times.

an enemy in a seemingly strong position can be defeated.

The Trojan Horse

One of the best examples of the use of surprise and deception occurred during the siege of the city of Troy in 1183 BCE. The besieging Greeks had been unable to capture the city, located on the Mediterranean coast of Turkey, for 10 years and so resorted to deception. They built a huge wooden horse and filled it with troops. The rest of the Greek army then appeared to sail away. The Trojans, believing the Greeks had fled, dragged the horse into Troy. The Greeks inside the wooden horse then left their hiding place at night and opened the city's gates to their comrades who had returned. The city was captured because of the trick.

The Greek leaders were clever in their use of deception. However, despite the importance of generals, the main participants in war have always been the ordinary soldiers. It is they through their courage or cowardice that make up the human story of warfare down the ages.

Egypt and the Ancient Middle East

Around 2450 BCE in Mesopotamia (now Iraq) there is evidence that a battle was fought between two opposing armies. After this, much of what is known about the history of the Middle East concerns warfare and the clash of civilizations. The Sumerians and the Egyptians were among the first to develop military units and train men to be soldiers. The most feared army of the region developed from about 1250 BCE. This was the powerful war machine of the Assyrian Empire in what is now northern Iraq.

Sumeria in southern Mesopotamia and Egypt were the first two areas of human settlement to develop an urban civilization with written records. Some of their monuments mention wars but historians know little about what happened during them. The Sumerian records tell of King Sargon of Akkad, who reigned from 2371 to 2316 BCE. He fought 34 battles to create an empire that controlled much of Mesopotamia.

The Egyptian Pharaoh Ramses III (the large figure on the far right) takes on the "Sea Peoples" in about 1175 BCE.

THE BATTLE OF KADESH

In 1294 BCE Ramses II of Egypt invaded Hittite territory to capture the city of Kadesh on the Orontes River. His army consisted of four divisions: the Amurru, the Amun, the Re, and the Ptah.

While the Egyptians were crossing the Orontes, "defecting" Hittite spies told Ramses that the Hittite army was at Aleppo. In fact the Hittite king, Muwatallis, and his army were at Kadesh. Ramses believed the lies and went ahead with the Amun. The Amurru was deployed to guard the crossing for the Re and the Ptah.

Muwatallis then sent 2,500 chariots across the Orontes and attacked the Re as it crossed the river. The Hittite strike force routed the Re, but was in turn attacked by the Egyptian Amurru division.

The Amurru broke through the Hittites and joined Ramses and the Amun. Muwatallis released another 1,000 chariots from his reserve. These were defeated by the combined attack of the Amurru and the Amun. The next day Ramses withdrew across the Orontes because Muwatallis still had 30,000 fresh infantry ready to send into action.

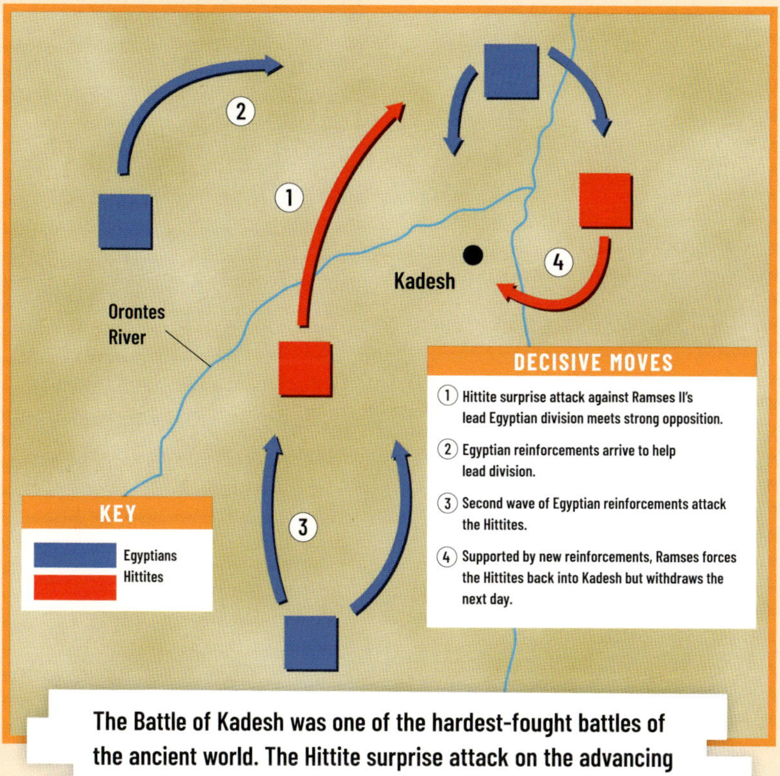

DECISIVE MOVES

1. Hittite surprise attack against Ramses II's lead Egyptian division meets strong opposition.
2. Egyptian reinforcements arrive to help lead division.
3. Second wave of Egyptian reinforcements attack the Hittites.
4. Supported by new reinforcements, Ramses forces the Hittites back into Kadesh but withdraws the next day.

The Battle of Kadesh was one of the hardest-fought battles of the ancient world. The Hittite surprise attack on the advancing Egyptians came close to success, but the Egyptians rallied and ended the battle in a slightly better position than the Hittites.

Nothing is known the campaigns of King Sargon of Akkad. Like most rulers of the time, he led his armies from the front and was expected to fight the enemy himself to win personal glory.

Caught by Surprise

An early battle that can be reconstructed in detail took place in 1469 BCE at Megiddo, in the north of what is now Israel, between Pharaoh Thutmosis III of Egypt and an alliance of Palestinian cities. The Palestinians expected the 20,000-strong Egyptian army to attack and had deployed their forces in a strong defensive position. Thutmosis, however, advanced from an unexpected direction, catching his opponents by surprise. The Palestinians lost their biggest advantage. Thutmosis won an overwhelming victory against the Palestinians. His victory made Egypt the dominant power in the ancient Middle East for a generation.

However, apart from evidence of some Egyptian battles, very little detailed information about the ancient Middle East's military history between the beginnings of Egyptian civilization in about 3000 BCE and about 750 BCE has survived. For example, archeologists are only able to reconstruct the barest outline of warfare between 1800 and 1600 BCE. Before this time armies were largely made up of undertrained foot soldiers—infantry. They might be armed with bows, slings, clubs, or spears. Bronze was used to make weapons, and armor, if worn at all, was made from leather, wicker, wood, or quilted cloth.

Ramses II leads the Egyptian chariots in a thunderous charge against the Hittites during the Battle of Kadesh in 1294 BCE. The lions have been added by the artist for dramatic effect!

Horse-drawn chariots came to briefly dominate the battlefield. They were brought to the Middle East by invading tribes from the north, such as the Hyksos who conquered and dominated Egypt between 1800 and 1600 BCE.

WARFARE IN THE ANCIENT MIDDLE EAST

The political geography of the ancient Middle East at the height of the Egyptian Empire.

The most famous battle between armies of chariots occurred at Kadesh in 1294 BCE between Ramses II of Egypt and the Hittite Empire. The battle was, in fact, a draw but Kadesh was noteworthy for the Hittites' use of iron weapons, while the Egyptians used bronze. Iron was harder than bronze and could be worked into a much sharper cutting edge.

The Aim of Warfare

The Hittites lived in central Asia Minor and for two centuries they were Egypt's main rival for control of that part of the Mediterranean coast now called Palestine (then called Canaan) and Syria. The Hittites also fought several wars in Syria against the Mitanni from northern Mesopotamia. These wars were fought to gain tribute from smaller states. The Egyptian strategy toward Palestine illustrates the aims and intentions of warfare at the time.

The Egyptians established their authority over Palestine during the reign of Amenhotep III (1390–1353 BCE). In each city they conquered

CHARIOT WARFARE

Horse-drawn chariots relied on speed in combat. Lines of chariots would race toward the enemy, the bow-armed crew shooting arrows rapidly. This kind of attack could cause heavy casualties among tight-packed masses of infantry who wore no armor. They could not run fast enough to catch the chariots or to get away from them.

The chariots were spaced far enough apart to allow them to turn. This allowed two lines charging one another to pass through each other's formation. As they passed each other, the crews would throw spears or shoot arrows.

Because horses were far more difficult to replace than men, and were very valuable if captured, both sides aimed at the smaller targets of the crew instead. But the shaking of the chariot as it bounced along over rough ground did not allow very accurate missile fire.

The chariots were fragile vehicles. The long pole to which the horses were harnessed was easily damaged and was difficult to replace. Both crews and horses had to be trained to a high degree.

the Egyptians placed a small garrison, which was fed and paid for by the people of the city. The cities also sent an annual sum of money or amount of produce to the Egyptian pharaoh. The cities could appeal to the pharaoh to help them in their disputes. The pharaoh would sometimes allow the Egyptian garrison to join with a city's army in an attack on a neighboring city.

The Sea Peoples

In 1200 BCE, about 500 years after the Hyksos swept through the ancient Middle East, a similar migration of people took place. This time, however, they came by sea. The Egyptians called these enemies the Sea Peoples. The Sea Peoples at first attacked the Hittites and destroyed their empire forever. Then they moved south and fought a naval battle off the coast of Egypt in 1189 BCE. The Egyptian fleet was victorious, however, and the Sea Peoples scattered throughout the Mediterranean. Some of them settled in Canaan and it is thought that the people known as the Philistines in the Bible may have been these same Sea Peoples.

The greatest military power of the ancient Middle East was Assyria. The people of Assur broke away from their Mitanni rulers under the leadership of Ashur-Uballit. In the following centuries they fought the Hittites. The first Assyrian army reached the coast of the Mediterranean during the reign of Tiglath-Pileser I (1120–1093 BCE).

The Assyrian Empire

Attacks by Aramean nomads from Babylonia in southern Mesopotamia halted the Assyrian expansion around 1050 BCE. Assyria only recovered during

TIGLATH-PILESER III AND THE ASSYRIAN ARMY

Before Tiglath-Pileser III became king of Assyria in 745 BCE, the Assyrian army was probably a part-time militia. These soldiers had to serve the king for a certain number of days each year and then returned to their civilian lives. Tiglath-Pileser III created four different categories of soldiers. The core of his military forces was a trained, full-time army.

First, there were the guards of the king, the queen, and the crown prince. Most were cavalry or chariots, with an infantry unit known as the "Heroes."

The second category was the King's Standing Army. These soldiers wore uniforms and were recruited from all the different peoples of the empire. In peacetime the King's Standing Army garrisoned towns and cities throughout the empire. The King's Standing Army included chariots, cavalry, and infantry.

Third, there were the King's Men, a militia like the army before Tiglath-Pileser's reforms. Some served as laborers.

The fourth group, consisting of all the other able-bodied men in the empire, made up the General Levy. This was used in times of national emergency.

Assyrian troops attack a city. The archer is protected by a large shield held by his assistant spearman.

the reigns of later kings. The Assyrians invaded Babylonia, Iran, and eastern Asia Minor. But after the death of Shalmaneser III (824 BCE) civil war in Assyria enabled cities to rebel against the Assyrians.

Like the Egyptians the Assyrians did not establish direct political control over the lands they conquered. They demanded tribute of livestock, food, and slaves from their subjects. Any city that attempted to rebel was subject to savage reprisals, such as the mass execution of its citizens. The use of these bloodthirsty terror tactics against civilians was a regular—and feared—Assyrian tactic.

The era of Assyrian weakness that followed the death of Shalmaneser III only ended in 745 BCE. In that year an Assyrian general called Pulu became king and took the name Tiglath-Pileser III. He reorganized the Assyrian government system and the army. Particular attention was paid to training, weaponry, siege warfare, and supply. It has been estimated that the Assyrians could put an army of about 100,000 men in the field, a huge figure by the standards of the day, and keep it supplied.

By the time of Tiglath-Pileser III's death in 727 BCE Assyria's frontiers were safe thanks to annual military campaigns against neighboring cities and kingdoms.

Attacked by Chariots

The Assyrian ruler Sennacherib left detailed descriptions of his military campaigns, which archeologists discovered when they excavated his palace at Nineveh, the Assyrian capital. The first battle of his reign took place in 703 BCE against a Babylonian army at Kish in Mesopotamia. Sennacherib's tactics combined chariots and cavalry. His chariots attacked the enemy's front and his cavalry attacked the flanks. Both used archery to kill or disrupt the enemy. These clever tactics won a total victory at a time when most battles were little more than uncontrolled brawls and were often indecisive.

In 702 BCE the Assyrians campaigned in the north. In this mountainous, forested countryside their chariots could not operate effectively, unlike on the flat plains of Babylonia. Sennacherib relied on his infantry and cavalry to impose his rule. The following year Sennacherib attacked an alliance of Palestinian rulers, who were supported by soldiers from Egypt.

The alliance fell apart. Its members were terrified at the possibility of Assyrian reprisals. Sidqa, the Philistine king of Ashkelon, was deported to Assyria with his family. One major battle between Egyptian and Assyrian armies ended in a victory for Sennacherib, who "personally captured alive the Egyptian charioteers with their prince," according to his own accounts.

Experts in Siege Warfare

During this campaign Sennacherib also besieged an important fortress controlled by the kingdom of Judah. A relief sculpture from his palace at Nineveh shows how the siege was done. Assyrian soldiers first built a large ramp of earth up to one of the walls of the fortress. They then wheeled battering rams up the ramp to punch a hole in the wall.

Behind the rams Assyrian bowmen kept the defenders' heads down with their archery. The archers sheltered behind wicker shields taller than themselves and with a curve at the top to protect them from the arrows shot by bowmen on the fortress's walls. The Assyrians also used great wooden siege towers that allowed their troops to reach the top of the enemy walls. The wall relief also shows the horrific aftermath of the siege—members of the garrison were impaled on stakes by the Assyrians.

The Assyrians were highly successful in siege warfare. This wall carving shows an Assyrian archer (protected by a shield bearer) shooting at a city's defenders while a covered battering ram moves up a ramp to smash into the wall. At the rear are executed enemy soldiers, impaled on stakes.

Years of constant warfare and resentment against the terror tactics used against the garrison in Judah—and many others— finally brought about the downfall of the Assyrian Empire. The empire reached its height during the reign of Ashurbanipal (688–625 BCE), when it controlled the entire ancient Middle East, including Egypt. But in 626 BCE the Babylonians rebelled and allied with the Medes of northwestern Iran, another people conquered by the Assyrians. In 612 BCE Nineveh was captured and destroyed by the rebels. A new phase in military history was about to begin, one centering on the newly emerging Persian Empire.

Persia Invades Greece

In the middle of the sixth century BCE the ruler of the Persians, a people who lived in the west of what is now Iran, embarked on a set of conquests that established the largest empire the world had yet seen. It included the area of what is now Turkey. Greek-speakers who lived on the west coast of Turkey in an area called Ionia slowly became hostile to their Persian overlords, sparking a prolonged war that saw the Persian Empire unleash its huge armies against mainland Greece. The Greeks fought back to maintain their freedom.

To the Greeks of Ionia there was at first no difference between their new Persian and their former overlords. Both demanded tribute, which the Greeks paid. However, the Persians gradually replaced the councils of rich local citizens that ruled the Ionian Greek cities with individuals who ruled like dictators. Nevertheless, it took some 50 years before the Ionians rebelled against their Persian rulers.

During this time the Persians conquered the rest of the Middle East. They took Mesopotamia, Egypt, and the lands to the west of Iran under their rule. They even invaded

A Greek (carrying a large shield bearing the emblem of the winged horse, Pegasus) and a Persian soldier fight each other. The wars fought between Greece and Persia are well documented in Greek histories and literature. There are still gaps in our knowledge but we have information about all the major encounters.

THE HOPLITE

The power of the Greek armies that fought the Persians rested in their armored foot soldiers called hoplites. Greek soldiers paid for their own military equipment. The wealthiest of them were armed with a spear about 10 feet (3 m) long, a bronze chest and back protector known as a corselet, a helmet, and a large, round shield. This was about 3 feet (0.92 m) in diameter and was known as a hoplon, from which the soldiers took their name.

The hoplites fought in close ranks, each man occupying about 3 feet (0.92 m). The shield of one protected the body of his neighbor to his left. The formation was known as a phalanx, from the Greek word for "roller."

The hoplites advanced relatively slowly toward the enemy. As long as they maintained their formation, their shields provided excellent protection against an enemy shooting arrows or thrusting spears. However, if the phalanx was attacked in the flanks or the hoplites had difficulty in keeping their formation across rough ground, the formation would break up and they would be defeated.

Europe, taking control of Thrace and Macedonia to the north of Greece and sending expeditions north of the Black Sea into the steppes of what is now Ukraine. It was the largest empire in the world at that time. The Persian rulers could draw on huge reserves of manpower.

Call for Help

In 499 BCE the wealthy city of Miletus in the south of Ionia was the first city to declare its independence. Other cities quickly followed. They formed a federation led by a congress made up of representatives from each. The Ionian Greeks knew they were not strong enough to defeat the Persian Empire. Their army barely numbered 10,000 while the Persian emperor, Darius, could easily summon 100,000 soldiers. The Ionian Greeks decided to ask other Greeks for help.

Revolt Begins

The ancient Greeks thought of themselves as one community, even though they lived in many separate city-states scattered across Sicily, southern Italy, the Greek mainland, Asia Minor, southern Russia, and even North Africa. They believed themselves to be united by their common language. They called anyone who spoke differently a barbarian because their languages sounded like "bar-bar-bar" to Greek ears. The Ionians hoped that their fellow Greek-speakers would help them gain their independence from the Persian "barbarians." However, only Athens and Eretria, a city on the Aegean island of Euboea, agreed to help the hard-pressed Ionians. They added only a few hundred soldiers to the Ionian army.

The Ionians, with their Athenian and Eretrian allies, attacked Sardis, the capital of the Persian province, or satrapy, of Lydia, in 498 BCE.

They drove the Persian governor, or satrap, out of the city. During the fighting Sardis burned to the ground. Although there is no proof that the Greeks burned it deliberately, Darius held the Athenians responsible.

Darius decided to avenge this insult but first he had to crush the Ionian revolt. As the Ionian army marched home from Sardis, the Persians attacked and defeated it. The Persian soldiers then laid siege to the Ionian cities. The Ionians were able to bring supplies by sea, however, and this allowed them to continue to resist the Persian attempts to capture their cities.

At the same time as the Ionian army had marched against Sardis, an Ionian fleet sailed to Cyprus. The island's capture would keep the Persians from using the Phoenician fleet (the best in the Mediterranean at that time) directly against Ionia. The Phoenicians were a trading nation from what is now Syria, Lebanon, and Israel. The whole of Cyprus except one city joined the Ionians, but the Persians were able to land on the island.

Persian Invasion

Although the Ionians defeated the Phoenicians in a sea battle, the Persians defeated the Cypriot rebels on land. The Ionian navy alone, despite its victory, could not prevent the Persians from reconquering the Cypriot cities. The Persian success against the Ionians on Cyprus in 498 BCE made sure that they would defeat the revolt. Although it took four years of hard fighting, they had restored their rule over the Ionian Greeks by 494 BCE.

Darius now prepared to invade mainland Greece itself. In 492 BCE, he sent a large army and navy to the

THE PERSIAN MILITARY SYSTEM

The Persians' control of a huge empire enabled them to field very large armies. Herodotus, a Greek historian who wrote about the Persian wars, claimed that over a million soldiers took part in the fighting. This was an exaggeration, but the Persians could easily bring together an army of more than 100,000 men recruited from the 20 provinces of their empire.

The best troops were those recruited in Persia itself and those from the warlike Scythian tribes to the north of the empire. The Persian infantry relied on their powerful bows made from layers of animal horn and wood. They also carried spears and light shields. The shield could be rested against the spear to create a barricade. The archers fired their arrows at an enemy formation to prepare the way for an attack.

At the same time horse archers from Scythia rode around the flanks and rear of the enemy formation shooting arrows all the time. When the enemy had been disorganized by the archery, the infantry picked up their spears and shields and joined Persian cavalry armed with short spears in a charge on the enemy.

Persian archers on a frieze made from ceramic tiles. Persian infantry did not wear heavy armor. They carry bows made from a mixture of wood, animal sinew, and horn, plus spears.

north of the Aegean Sea under the command of his son-in-law, Mardonius. Mardonius planned to invade Greece but a storm wrecked most of his ships. Mardonius withdrew, but Darius was soon planning another full-scale invasion of Greece. In 490 BCE a large fleet carrying 20,000 Persian soldiers left Ionia and attacked the island of Naxos and then the city of Eretria on the island of Euboea. The Persians captured Eretria and destroyed the city. They sold its inhabitants into slavery.

A Greek illustration of a hoplite soldier from the fifth century BCE. His helmet is by his side. The image clearly shows how hoplites gripped their shields.

From Eretria the Persians sailed for Athenian territory, landing near the town of Marathon. The Athenians gathered together their army to fight.

When the Athenian army of 9,000 soldiers reached Marathon, they waited for a few days before attacking. The Persians decided to divide their forces, putting some soldiers back on their ships to sail from Marathon to Athens while the rest advanced by land. But before the Persians could put their plan into operation the Athenians attacked. The Greeks carried out a brilliant encircling maneuver. They killed about a third of the Persian army and burned many ships. The surviving Persians then decided to return to Ionia.

So great and unexpected was the Greek victory that a messenger, Pheidippides, ran the 26 miles (41 km) from Marathon to Athens to announce the triumph. His great feat is still commemorated today in the Olympic marathon race.

Darius decided that he would have to conquer all of Greece. However, he died in 485 BCE, delaying the next Persian expedition. Xerxes succeeded Darius as Persian emperor. In 480 BCE Xerxes assembled an army and used a bridge of boats to cross the Hellespont, the stretch of water separating Europe from Asia Minor.

The city-states of Greece formed a league against the Persians. Sparta, which had the most powerful army, was the leader of the league. The Greeks chose to place an army at Thermopylae. This narrow pass, with mountains on one side and the sea on the other, would stop he Persians from outflanking the small Greek army.

Fighting to the Last Man

After three days of fighting the Persian army destroyed the Greek forces guarding Thermopylae. Xerxes discovered that a narrow trail led over a mountain. His troops were able to get behind the Greek position. He sent 1,000 of his best soldiers to follow this path while others attacked the Greeks from the front. All of the Spartans died rather than surrender.

The Persians advanced into central Greece. They captured and burned Athens, but the Athenians had evacuated their entire population. The Persian dream of avenging the burning of Sardis was nearly fulfilled but a crushing naval defeat in the Bay of Salamis destroyed their fleet.

The Persian army remained powerful, however. A large force remained in Greece to resume the campaign in 479 BCE.

The Persian and Greek armies met in the decisive Battle of Plataea, northwest of Athens. Mardonius, the Persian commander, attempted to force the Greeks to fight on a flat plain, where the Persian cavalry would be effective. When the Greeks tried to change their position, Mardonius believed they were fleeing. He attacked with his army but the Greeks were better at fighting hand-to-hand.

A reconstruction of an Athenian trireme. These ships won the Battle of Salamis. Athenian seamanship, tactics, and warships were superior to those of the Persians.

THE BATTLE OF SALAMIS

The decisive battle of Xerxes' campaign in Greece occurred at Salamis in 480 BCE. To conquer all Greece, it was necessary for the Persians to cross the narrow Isthmus of Corinth. Thermopylae had already proved that the Persians needed larger numbers to defeat a Greek army. On the Isthmus of Corinth they would need a fleet to land troops behind the Greek defenses.

After the city of Athens had been destroyed by the Persians, the Athenian admiral Themistocles sent a message to Xerxes, saying that the Athenians would change sides when the Persians attacked the Greek fleet based at Salamis.

To attack, the Persians would have to sail through a narrow channel between the island and the mainland. Themistocles, however, had lied. The Athenians did not change sides. Although both fleets were able to fit 80 ships across the width of the channel, the Greek formation was three lines deep, while that of the Persian was ten lines deep. The Persian superiority in numbers was meaningless. The Greek navy destroyed the Persian fleet.

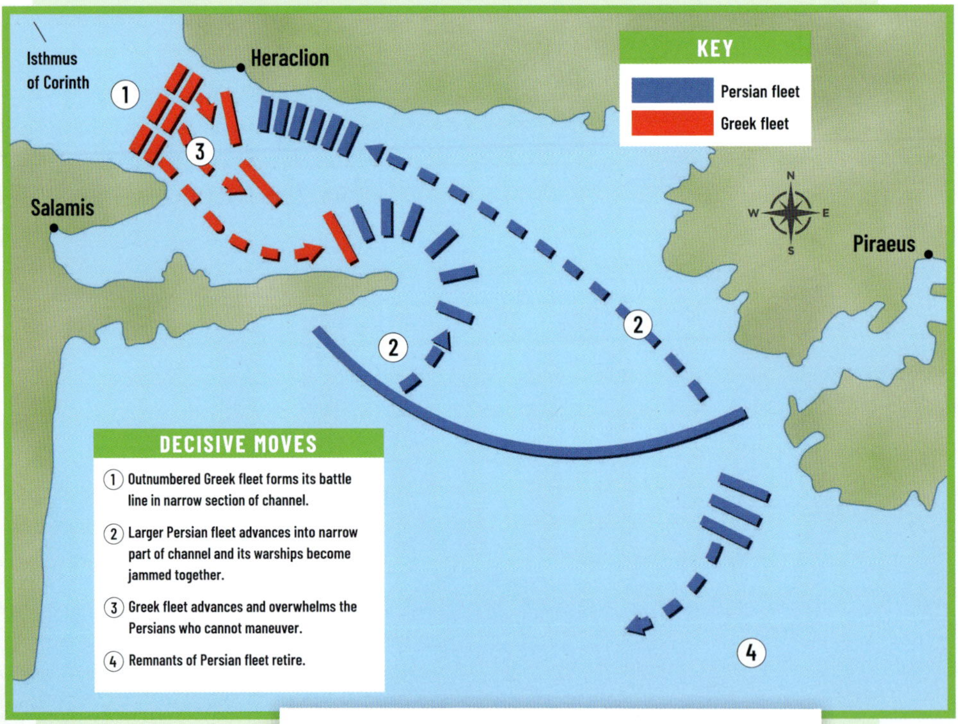

The Battle of Salamis cost the Persians half their fleet—around 350 vessels. The Greeks lost only 40 ships during the naval victory.

Greek hoplites (on the right) advance steadily against the Persians at the Battle of Plataea. The Greek victory was total. Around 50,000 Persians were reported as killed, while Greek losses amounted to fewer than 1,500 according to writers at the time. The battle was won due to the better military skills shown by the Greeks.

The Persians were defeated and Mardonius himself was killed. A few weeks later a Greek fleet that had sailed across the Aegean Sea to Mycale in Ionia defeated the Persian army and fleet there. The Ionian Greeks, who were supposedly part of the Persian imperial armed forces, switched sides as the battle began. After the Greek victories of 479 BCE Ionia became part of the anti-Persian Delian League, which was led by Athens.

Egypt Rebels

This alliance continued the war against Persia until 448 BCE. Its strategy was to liberate all the Greek cities around the Aegean. In 466 BCE a Delian League fleet defeated the Persians at the Battle of the Eurymedon River on the coast of Asia Minor. The year afterward Xerxes died and Egypt rebelled against Persian rule. It took 10 years for the Persians to reconquer Egypt. The length of the struggle was in part thanks to the 200 ships sent by the Athenians in 459 BCE to help the rebels against the Persians.

In 448 BCE the Athenians and Persians came to an agreement called the Peace of Callias after the chief Athenian negotiator. The wars between Persia and Greece ended, but suspicion between Greeks and Persians continued.

Athens Against Sparta

Victory over the Persian army at Plataea in 479 BCE had saved Greece from invasion by the Persian empire. Having united in the face of attack from outside, however, the Greek city states began to fight amongst themselves. In particular there was division between Athens and Sparta. Each side had different governing systems and built up separate alliances. Athens used its powerful navy to create a broad sphere of influence across the Aegean Sea, while Sparta was more powerful on land. War was inevitable.

The Spartan hoplite phalanx was the best in the Greek world. The ferocious discipline that ran like a thread through all Spartan life ensured its battlefield supremacy. The mothers of Spartan hoplites told their sons departing for battle to return victorious with their shields, or as corpses upon them. The rich Athenians, by contrast, could afford a powerful navy. The equipment of a hoplite was costly and only land-owning farmers could afford armor, shield, and spear. All that was needed to crew an Athenian war galley—the trireme, a wooden warship with three banks of oars—were strong backs and arms to pull the oars.

A peltast, a light infantry soldier. Peltasts carried lighter equipment than the hoplites and were able to maneuver around the enemy phalanx, using their throwing spears to disrupt it.

THRACIAN AND GREEK WARFARE

The ancient Greeks did not think of nationality in the way we do today. To them a Greek was someone who spoke the language. A barbarian was everyone else. This stern view excluded Thrace, an area that is now part of modern Greece. Despite this, the Thracians had a profound impact on the way Greeks waged war. The main troop type in a Thracian army was a peltast, named after the shield the man carried, the pelte. A peltast fought in a hit-and-run manner, throwing javelins from a distance, springing ambushes, and avoiding hand-to-hand combat. The first record of mercenary Thracian peltasts in the Greek world was in Athens around 540 BCE. They were employed by the dictator Pisistratus. By 350 BCE many Greek city-states, such as Aetolia and Phocaea, used peltast methods of fighting. The word peltast soon became used interchangeably with the word for a mercenary soldier.

Tension with Athens

Sparta dominated the Greek world after Persia's defeat. It had played a major part in the victory over Persia at Plataea in 479 BCE that had driven the invaders out of Greece. However, the tension with Athens grew out of its victory over the Persians at Mycale the same year. This Athenian victory made sure that the Persians did not have a fleet to invade Greece, a peninsula dominated by the sea.

While Sparta was content to drive the Persians out of Greece, Athens carried on the war. It was determined to liberate the Greek cities of Asia Minor's western coast from Persian rule. The Athenians won a string of naval victories. These both increased the prestige of Athens among the freed cities and created an alliance, the Delian League (see page 23), that looked to Athens for leadership. As the Delian League grew in importance, Sparta was losing its position as the most powerful Greek state.

Athens and its allies signed a peace treaty with Persia in 448 BCE. However, Athens and Sparta were already at war. The conflict became known as the First Peloponnesian War. This began as a war between Athens and Sparta's ally Corinth in 460 BCE. Sparta joined in three years later, defeated Athens at the Battle of Tanagra, and then withdrew. The war concluded in a deadlock in 445 BCE but it heralded a period known as the Thirty Years Peace. The peace did not, however, last for 30 years.

Walls of Piraeus

During the war the Athenians had built a pair of walls that linked Athens with its port on the coast, Piraeus. This meant that Athens could withstand a long siege. Supplies brought by ship could be carried into the city along the road between the walls. Building these walls was a shrewd move by the Athenians. Sieges in the ancient world took a long time. What an invading army needed to do was make an enemy come out from behind its walls and fight in the open. Starvation was one option.

Commanders usually planned invasions to take place at about the time of the annual harvest. The grain in the fields would burn easily and the work of a year could be lost. A winter of famine was the likely result. Next year's harvest could also be ruined if all the seeds had been destroyed. It was important to defeat an invading army in battle before it could rampage through the countryside.

The Athenian navy, the world's best at the time, and the walls to the port meant there was no need for the Athenian hoplites to fight their Spartan counterparts in the open. Grain could be shipped into Piraeus, watched over by the Athenian fleet. There would be no famine. Nor would the citizen-soldiers of Sparta want to conduct a lengthy siege. They had their own crops to harvest back home.

The Thirty Years Peace ended in 431 BCE. Athens and Sparta's ally Corinth had already fought a naval battle near the island of Corfu and a land battle at Potidaea, a small town in the northeast of Greece. These provided the Spartans with an excuse to go to war. The war that followed lasted for 20 years, with a brief period of peace between 421 and 414 BCE.

Indirect Approach to War

The first notable change in the war related to strategy. The Athenians knew they faced a long struggle, but the Spartans expected the war would be a short one. This

CIVIL WARS OF ANCIENT GREECE

The civil wars of ancient Greece were fought mainly around the coast of the eastern Mediterranean and the Greek mainland.

THE SICILIAN EXPEDITION

Between 447 and 440 BCE the army of Athens intervened in a war between the Greek cities of Sicily. Athens wanted to ruin their grain trade. The planned intervention failed, but when a new war broke out in Sicily in 415 BCE, the Athenians chose to intervene again.

They sent an army and powerful fleet to attack Syracuse, the most important Greek city on the island. The expedition was a disaster. Divided leadership and a too-careful approach made sure the Syracusans had ample warning of the attack. A siege that lasted two years began. Just as the Athenians were on the point of success, the Spartans and Corinthians arrived on the scene.

In 413 BCE defeats in Syracuse's harbor and a disastrous night attack against the city's defenses caused the Athenians to give up the siege. Their army was destroyed as it retreated. Athens never regained the upper hand in the conflict. The Sicilian Expedition had been a disaster.

was partly because they did not understand the importance of the walls from Athens to Piraeus.

Pericles, the chief Athenian political leader, convinced the citizens that they had to send expeditions of ships and hoplites to attack Sparta's allies from the sea. The Athenians hoped that the cost of a prolonged war would be too much for Sparta's allies to bear. This "indirect" approach to warfare was a new strategy. Previous wars had been usually won or lost in a single, decisive battle.

The Spartans attempted to counter this strategy, which the Athenians followed throughout the war, by building a fortress on Athenian territory, at Decelea, in 413 BCE. Instead of being confined to seasonal raids at harvest time, they could now attack Athenian farms all year round.

The second change concerned naval warfare. The Athenians had developed their skill with the trireme to a high level. They no longer needed to board enemy vessels and fight hand-to-hand. They were able to use their own galleys as weapons in their own right, rather than as a fighting platform for land soldiers.

New Naval Tactics

They sailed their triremes in a formation known as the "line ahead." Squadrons of 10 or 20 triremes followed the changes in course of the lead galley in the line. This allowed them to carry out more sophisticated, coordinated maneuvers than were possible with the traditional line abreast, in which galleys lined up side by side.

The Athenian methods allowed the best use of the ram, which was placed at the bow of a galley just below the waterline. The Athenians often outmaneuvered enemy naval squadrons, placing their triremes in positions from where they could use the ram to smash through the sides of the opposing war galleys. A naval victory by an Athenian admiral, Phormio, in the Gulf of Patras in 429 BCE best illustrates the high degree of skill possessed by Athenian oarsmen. Phormio was faced by a Corinthian fleet that had more galleys but was transporting troops. Carrying more men than usual, as well as a lot of heavy equipment and supplies, made the Corinthian ships less maneuverable. In the early morning of the day of battle the Athenians caught up with the Corinthians. The Corinthians formed a circle, with the bows of their galleys facing outward toward the Athenian fleet. This formation was the traditional defensive pattern in Greek naval warfare and had usually worked well in the past.

The Athenians, sailing in line ahead, began to circle the Corinthian ships at a distance. This left room for the Athenians to dodge any attempts to ram them, as it would take some time for the enemy oarsmen to reach ramming speed. Phormio waited for the morning easterly wind to blow. This made the water more choppy. The Corinthians became disorganized. Phormio then destroyed the Corinthian fleet, capturing a quarter of its ships.

A New Type of Soldier

It was a third development that had the greatest impact on Greek warfare. The phalanx worked well on flat ground. However, a phalanx moved slowly to keep its order and could be disordered by rough terrain. In 426 BCE an Athenian army fighting in the rugged terrain of western Greece faced Aetolian soldiers who carried lighter shields and javelins.

The Athenian general Demosthenes attempted to chase after the Aetolians but they easily outran the phalanx. The Aetolians kept their distance and threw their javelins until the tired, wounded hoplites could no longer keep their formation. The Aetolians then charged, killing many of the hoplites. Demosthenes survived this defeat and learned a harsh lesson. In his next battle he hid a mixed force of hoplites and light infantry, known as peltasts (see page 25), in a gully. When the larger enemy force advanced past the gully, Demosthenes' troops attacked them from the rear. Combining different types of soldier, the Athenians won a major victory.

The Athenian force is attacked from all sides as it retreats from Syracuse at the end of the siege of the city during the disastrous Sicilian Expedition.

"ONE STEP MORE"

The Theban general Epaminondas demonstrated his genius at the Battle of Leuctra in 371 BCE. His new technique was using the oblique order. He also took to its logical extreme another aspect of hoplite warfare.

When phalanxes met in battle, the front ranks each tried to force their way into the enemy formation. Men in the rear ranks placed their shields against the backs of those in front and shoved to create gaps in the enemy line.

Epaminondas more than doubled the normal depth of a phalanx. This gave his troops a momentum that allowed them to crash into the ranks of their opponents. Within moments at Leuctra the Spartan command was wiped out. With a cry of "One step more" Epaminondas's phalanx surged forward and destroyed the reputation of Spartan military supremacy.

Demosthenes continued to use peltasts at the battles of Idomene and Sphacteria in 425 BCE. He also took part in an Athenian expedition to the island of Sicily between 415 and 413 BCE. Despite his best efforts the Athenians were defeated—by peltasts. Another Athenian general, Iphicrates, became an expert in the tactics of light infantry and ambush. His greatest victories using peltasts and ambushes were over Sparta at Lechaion in 393 BCE and Abydus in 388 BCE.

The Sacred Band

Iphicrates' victories occurred during a series of wars the Greek world fought between 400 and 362 BCE. Athens and other city-states challenged the supremacy that Sparta had won during the Peloponnesian Wars. During these wars Epaminondas, a general from the city of Thebes to the northwest of Athens, made the last truly great tactical innovation of ancient Greek hoplite warfare.

At the Battle of Leuctra in 371 BCE Epaminondas took advantage of a feature of hoplite battles to make the first recorded use of the oblique order. Hoplite armies formed their phalanx with the best troops on the far right of the battle line. Epaminondas placed his best troops—called the Sacred Band—on the left instead. He then advanced in a staggered line, which meant that his best troops met the enemy first. The troops following behind protected the Sacred Band's unshielded flank. This oblique order overwhelmed the Spartans at Leuctra.

Hoplite armies of the Greek wars were transformed by experiences gained in war. A Greek army of 356 BCE was very different from one at the end of the civil wars. But the Greeks were about to meet another army that had absorbed these lessons. The Macedonian army of Philip II and his son, Alexander the Great, would win great victories in Greece, the Middle East, and beyond.

The Conquests of Alexander the Great

During the fifth and early fourth centuries BCE, Macedonia, a country to the north of the Greek peninsula, was a minor power in ancient Greece. Its weakness lay in the inability of its kings to enforce their rule over the powerful nobles who lived in the north of the country. In 359 BCE a new ruler, Philip II, took power there. He curbed the influence of the nobles and created one of the greatest armies of the ancient world. Philip's son, Alexander the Great, would use this army to carve out an enormous empire.

Philip of Macedon's army crushes the Athenians at the decisive Battle of Chaeronea in 338 BCE. The battle made Macedonia the most important and powerful state on the Greek mainland.

ALEXANDER THE GREAT

Alexander the Great remains one of the outstanding commanders in all history. He won decisive victories in four major battles: the Granicus River in 334 BCE, Issus in 333 BCE, Arbela in 331 BCE, and the Hydaspes River in 326 BCE. He captured Tyre, the strongest fortress-city in the ancient world, in 332 BCE.

In a number of smaller conflicts he triumphed over barbarian hill tribes, Scythian horse-archers, and Indian armies of elephants and chariots. No other general in history consistently succeeded against so many different opponents. He was also often heavily outnumbered.

Alexander's courage set an example for the rest of his army to follow. He always fought in the front rank and suffered some terrible wounds during his campaigns. However, his heroism was the product of a violent nature.

He ordered that a loyal general and a servant be murdered because they objected to his administrative policies. While drunk and angry, Alexander also stabbed to death one of his boyhood friends.

Alexander the Great's life was a short one, but he still carved out a vast empire.

Although no one realized it at first, Philip II's reforms began a process of change in the warfare of ancient Greece. This was a change that would be exploited to the full by his brilliant son, Alexander. Because Macedonia was a kingdom and the king commanded the army, it had the same leadership for several campaigns in a row.

The Greek city-states, by comparison, changed their generals ever year or two. This would not have made any difference if Philip and his successors had been poor leaders. However, they were great leaders with a genius for warfare. They also had the best army. Philip was determined to make Macedonia the most powerful state in Greece.

SIEGE WARFARE TECHNIQUES

Unless an ancient army could capture a city or fortress by betrayal from inside, it faced a long siege. Either an opening had to be made in the walls using battering rams, or movable towers and scaling ladders were used to allow soldiers to climb up to the top of the walls.

One of the finest examples of siege warfare is Alexander's capture of Tyre, now in Lebanon. He arrived at the city, located on an island off the coast, in early 332 BCE. Alexander's first move was to bring his battering rams and towers to the walls of the city by constructing a large earthen roadway from the mainland. He also built ships that carried battering rams. These ships were anchored beside the walls of Tyre so Alexander could launch attacks from the sea.

The siege of the port of Tyre. Alexander personally led attacks on the walls and was badly wounded in one attack. It took eight months to capture the city.

Philip was ready to go to war to achieve his ambition. Macedonia already had some of the best cavalry of all the Greek armies, so Philip first concentrated his efforts on reforming the infantry. He gave them a new weapon, a pike—the sarissa—some 16 feet (4.9 m) long. It was a difficult weapon to use as it was heavy and required well-drilled soldiers to wield it effectively. Philip put more emphasis on training than the part-time militia armies of the city-states did. This training paid off in the many wars that followed.

In 358 BCE a war began between some of the cities of central Greece. The war was about control of an important Greek religious shrine at Delphi. The city-state of Phocis claimed it belonged to them. The people of Delphi disagreed, saying that they lived in neutral territory ruled by a council made up of representatives from across the whole of Greece.

The council declared war on Phocis and its allies, Athens and Sparta. Thebes, the most powerful of the Greek city-states, supported the council. A civil war in Thessaly, a kingdom between Macedonia and central Greece, complicated matters. Philip used this war to extend Macedonia's influence. He entered the war in 354 BCE. The Phocians had captured Delphi and used the treasures of the temple to pay for armies of mercenaries. They conquered much of central Greece and backed one side in the Thessalian civil war. The other Thessalian side asked Philip for help. Philip was at first defeated by the Phocians, who used stone throwing catapults on the battlefield for the first time in recorded history.

A Mercenary Army Destroyed

In 353 BCE Philip returned and destroyed the Phocian mercenary army. Philip went on to capture some towns in the north of Greece and gained control of Thessaly.

When the war ended in 346 BCE, a treaty between Macedonia and Athens acknowledged Macedonian power in the north. Macedonia even became a member of the council ruling Delphi in Phocis's place.

When the next major war in Greece began in 339 BCE, Thebes and Athens allied against Macedonia. The two armies met at Chaeronea in central Greece in 338 BCE. The Athenian and Theban army totaled 35,000 men. The Macedonians had 30,000 infantry and 2,000 cavalry. The battle was as much a triumph for Philip's son, Alexander, as it was for him. Alexander led the cavalry, which like Philip's infantry was armed with spears, or lances. Alexander's cavalry charge wiped out the elite Theban Sacred Band, and Philip's infantry killed or captured 3,000 Athenians.

The victory made Philip master of Greece. He created the Confederacy of Corinth and intended to use it to wage war on Persia. Philip was elected the Confederacy's chief general in 337 BCE and began assembling an army and navy with the aim of attacking the Persian empire.

Alexander's First Campaigns

In 336 BCE Philip was assassinated. Alexander, only 19 years old at the time, was now king. Alexander first had to establish his personal authority over Greece. He was a popular, and brave leader but was prone to violent bouts of rage, even against his oldest friends. He led the Macedonian army into Greece in order to force the Confederacy of Corinth to elect him general in his father's place. Then, in 335 BCE, he attacked tribes in Thrace and Illyria that were threatening Macedonia. In Greece itself, Thebes rebelled against Macedonian power in 335 BCE, Alexander besieged the town and had it razed to the ground when it surrendered as an example to the other city-states.

The following year Alexander crossed the Hellespont into Asia Minor (modern Turkey) with an army of 40,000 soldiers. The Persian governors of the provinces of Asia Minor attempted to stop him at the Granicus River, but Alexander used his numerical superiority and aggressive tactics to defeat their army.

Despite his victory at the Granicus River, Alexander was in a potentially dangerous situation. He was a long way from home, the Persians would be able to build a new army thanks to their huge reserves of manpower, and they still had a large, powerful navy. Alexander, displaying the strategic vision that was one of his greatest gifts, chose to deal with the Persian navy first.

Alexander's plan was simple but risky. He decided to capture the main Persian ports along the Mediterranean coast. Without

Alexander (center, with sword in hand) leads the Macedonian cavalry in a desperate charge against the Persians during the Battle of the Granicus River in May 334 BCE. It was his first great victory in Asia.

Alexander the Great is shown the body of the Persian emperor Darius III, who had fled after the climactic Battle of Arbela.

these the Persian fleet would have no bases to operate from and Alexander's lines of communication to Greece would be secure.

Alexander did not have a fleet so he planned to lay siege to the Persian ports. The Macedonians spent the next year capturing the coastal cities, except for that of Helicarnassus.

The Battle of Issus

In 333 BCE Alexander advanced inland into Syria to deal with a new Persian army. The Persian emperor, Darius III, had gathered an army of 100,000 soldiers and now led it to a position between Alexander's forces and Asia Minor. The Persians were trying to cut Alexander off from his homeland. Alexander had to turn his army around and march back to meet the Persians. At the Battle of Issus Alexander defeated Darius's army and almost killed the Persian emperor. Some 50,000 Persians were slaughtered. Alexander lost 450 men. Alexander, as usual, led his cavalry in a charge that cracked the Persian line and his infantry took advantage of the disorder. Darius fled the battlefield.

During the next two years Alexander conquered the Mediterranean coast of the Middle East and Egypt. His most difficult task was capturing the port of Tyre. Alexander placed the great port under siege in January 332 BCE, but it took him eight month to capture it. Alexander was cruel to its defenders and citizens. The city was destroyed and most of those inside were sold as slaves. His use of terror was deliberate—he hoped Tyre would serve as an example to other cities that dared defy him.

Darius, meanwhile, had assembled another large army recruited from the central and eastern provinces of his empire. Darius gathered his forces at Babylon in Mesopotamia. The final battle between Darius and Alexander took place at Arbela, about 300 miles (480 km) north of Babylon. Alexander won a crushing victory, although he was again massively outnumbered.

Alexander's War Machine

Alexander was undoubtedly a great general and certainly more than a match for his Persian enemies, despite being outnumbered in all his battles against them. However, Alexander had several advantages, not least the fact that his army was united. On the other hand, the Persian army was made up of men of many different nationalities, few of whom had much desire to die in battle for their Persian masters.

Also Alexander's army was professional, and had the best infantry and cavalry around. The cream of Alexander's mounted arm was the Companion cavalry. These were armored cavalrymen dressed in back- and breastplates, crested helmets, and leg greaves (armor). They carried a lance that could either be thrown or thrust at a target. Their secondary weapon was a short sword. Alexander usually led the Companion cavalry into battle, and few of his enemies were capable of resisting them. As the stirrup used to control a horse was not invented until the second century CE, and hard saddles did not begin to appear until the third century CE, the Companion cavalry had to train intensively to manage their horses in battle formations.

Alexander spent the three years after Arbela conquering Persia. Darius was eventually murdered by one of his own men.

The Persian emperor Darius (left-center, on a chariot) sees his army destroyed by a Macedonian cavalry charge. Alexander's Companion cavalry proved decisive at the Battle of Arbela.

THE BATTLE OF ARBELA

The Battle of Arbela (also known as Gaugamela) in 331 BCE shows how a general with an army of much smaller size can defeat an opponent with a larger one. Alexander the Great hoped that by attacking rapidly he could kill the enemy general before the larger enemy forces overwhelmed his army's flanks. He divided his army into three commands. His right wing was to advance quickly to engage the enemy left wing. Meanwhile, his left wing was to advance much more slowly and to the right. The center of Alexander's army advanced at a normal speed, also moving to its right. When the Persians realized what was happening, they attempted to move their army to the right to maintain their overlap.

This movement opened a gap in their line. When Alexander saw this, he charged toward it with his best troops, the lance-armed Companion cavalry. These broke through the Persian line, and Alexander continued their charge in the direction of Darius, the Persian emperor, who fled. Other Macedonian troops followed the cavalry and began rolling up the Persian line. Alexander's victory was total. The Persian empire had been conquered.

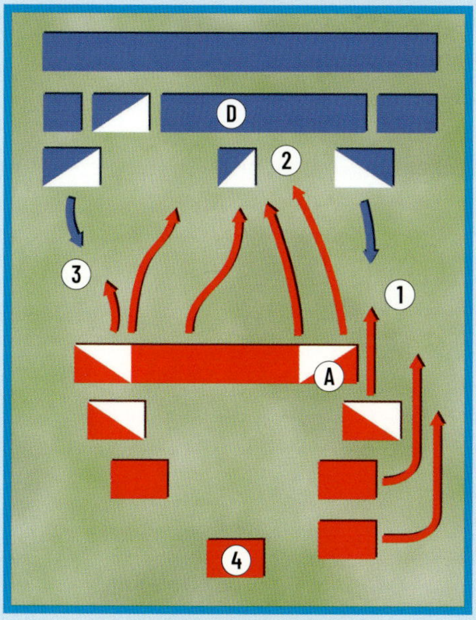

DECISIVE MOVES

1. Alexander's right wing charges and holds Persian left wing.
2. Alexander's center advances and smashes through gap in Persian front.
3. Persian attack on Macedonian left wing is finally defeated.
4. As Persian Army collapses, Macedonian reserves attack to complete the victory.

KEY

- Macedonian infantry
- Macedonian cavalry
- Persian cavalry
- Persian infantry
- (A) Alexander
- (D) Darius

Alexander's army of 47,000 men faced around 200,000 Persians at Arbela. Alexander decided to attack despite the odds believing, correctly as events turned out, that his men's discipline and training were far superior to those of the Persian army's infantry and cavalry.

Alexander proved himself to be a brilliant innovator on one occasion. His way forward was blocked by the Jaxartes River, the far bank of which was defended by the enemy. Alexander ordered his men to fill their tents with hay and sew them up, turning them into crude rafts. His soldiers then used these to float across the river. As they crossed, they were protected by their own archers. Alexander's victories made him the unquestioned emperor of the Middle East. However, he had still greater ambitions. In 327 BCE his army marched into India.

In May of the following year Alexander defeated an Indian army at the Battle of the Hydaspes River. Later in the campaign Alexander sent part of his army by sea under the command of his good friend Nearchus, demonstrating his ability to combine the movement of land and sea forces. Only a mutiny by his own troops prevented Alexander from continuing to campaign farther east.

Death of Alexander

In 324 BCE Alexander returned to Mesopotamia. He was faced with the immense task of ruling over an empire that stretched from Greece in the west to the Indus River in the east, and from the Jaxartes River in Central Asia to Egypt. But in 323 BCE he fell ill with a fever in

Indian king Porus awaits the Macedonian advance at the Battle of the Hydaspes River in 326 BCE. Alexander was heavily outnumbered and his troops also had to disable around 100 elephants. But again he was victorious.

ALEXANDER'S CAMPAIGNS

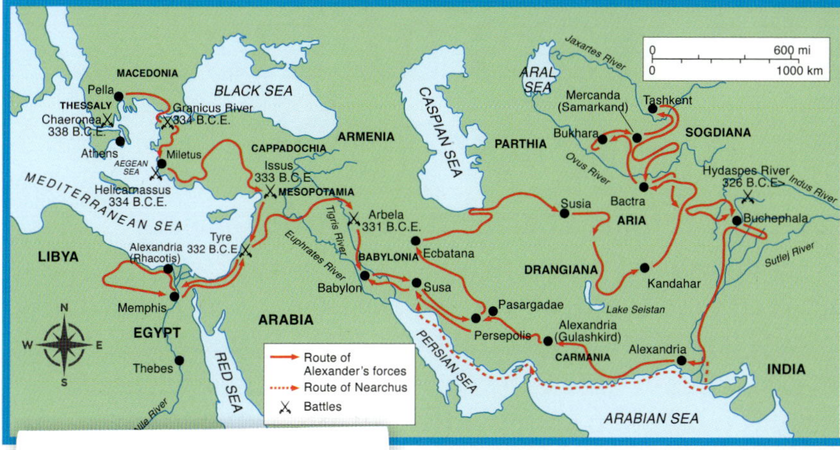

Alexander carved out a great empire throughout the Middle East but it collapsed after his death as his generals fought each other for power.

his capital Babylon and died. He was still only 33 years old. His death was unexpected, and the choice of his successor fell to the commanders of his army. Alexander's wife and son, the legitimate successor, were murdered by the commanders. With these two out of the way, the generals fought each other for power. The ruler Alexander had left in Macedonia, Antipater, refused to accept an empire run from Babylon. Between 321 and 281 BCE there were constant wars in the eastern Mediterranean.

Alexander's most senior successors were all soon dead. With them died any hope of keeping Alexander's empire as a single state. Instead of cooperating, the various generals were hungry for personal power and they chose to grab individual provinces and declare themselves kings. One of them, Ptolemy, did so in Egypt and established the longest-lasting dynasty of all of them.

Alexander's Empire Begins to Dissolve

Unstable and confusing alliances featured in all of these wars. In 301 BCE, after a battle in central Asia Minor, the three main empires in succession to Alexander's emerged. Ptolemy was king of Egypt, Antipater's son Cassander was ruler of Macedon, and a cavalry commander named Seleucus ruled Mesopotamia and Iran. Macedonia was briefly part of Seleucus's Seleucid Empire in 280 BCE but soon became independent.

The wars of the third century BCE between those who hoped to inherit Alexander's position decided very little in the Middle East. None of these bloody wars changed the dominance of Egypt, Macedonia, and the Seleucid dynasty. Their next great enemy would be Rome.

The Wars of the Roman Republic

In the fifth century BCE, Rome was just one of many city-states in the Italian peninsula. Italy itself was divided between Gauls in the north, the Etruscans who dominated central Italy, Latin speakers south of the Etruscans and several cities of Greek-speakers in the southeast. These peoples were often at war with each other. Rome was by no means the strongest state but it eventually defeated its rivals and began to extend its influence further over the Mediterranean world.

By 400 BC. Rome was a small city in the middle of a war with the Etruscan city of Veii to its north. The Romans had frequently been subject to Etruscan rule since the city of Rome's foundation in 753 BCE. The last war with Veii ended in 396 BCE and was a Roman victory. Rome's independence was finally secure. The Romans, however, had to face many more enemies.

Six years later a band of Gauls from the north invaded central Italy and ravaged the Etruscan lands. The Romans put their army into the field against the Gauls, but were

King Pyrrhus. He led an army that fought the Battle of Heraclea against Rome in 280 BCE. Pyrrhus, horrified by his losses at Heraclea, said: "One more such victory and I am lost."

THE ELEPHANT AT WAR

Indian armies used elephants in war from at least the sixth century BCE. Their widespread use in warfare in Europe and the Middle East only occurred after Alexander's campaigns there between 327 and 326 BCE. The army of the Seleucid Empire made the greatest use of them but they were used by many of the states of the Mediterranean during the second and third centuries BCE.

Elephants were usually placed in the first line of an army. They might open the battle with a charge that would crash into enemy troops. They might also be used against enemy cavalry in an army without elephants, as horses do not like an elephant's odor.

An elephant carried a crew of two to four soldiers armed with bows, javelins, or spears. A small tower was sometimes chained to the back of an elephant to give the crew greater protection.

The most successful tactic against elephants was to use light infantry fighting in open order and armed with javelins. They could swarm around the elephant, stabbing at its sensitive trunk or hind quarters. Wounded or maddened elephants would often crash into their own supporting troops.

themselves crushed by the Gauls at the Battle of the Allia River in 390 BCE. The Gauls captured and sacked Rome and only left the city after the Romans agreed to pay them money.

Not for the last time in their history, however, the Romans demonstrated their ability to recover from disaster. In 389 BCE they were again at war with neighboring cities. Roman success allowed them to create a Latin Confederacy that increased their military power. It also brought them into conflict with a neighboring people from central Italy known as the Samnites.

Change in Rome's Fortunes

Between 343 and 290 BCE the Romans and Samnites fought three wars. The most dramatic swings in fortune for Rome occurred during the second war. In 321 BCE the Romans suffered one of their most bitter defeats at the Battle of the Caudine Forks south of Rome. Their army was trapped between two barricades in a valley and starved into submission. After 311 BCE the Samnites always had an ally in their war with Rome, at first Etruscans, then the peoples of eastern Italy. The Romans defeated each in turn and won the decisive Battle of Bovianum in 305 BCE.

The third war's decisive battle occurred at Sentinum in 295 BCE, when the Romans defeated a combined army of Etruscans, Gauls, and Samnites. As the Roman army was faltering, one of its generals, Publius Decius Mus, deliberately sacrificed his own life to inspire his men to fight harder. The Samnites continued the war alone for five more years but in the end Rome

THE EARLY EXPANSION OF ROME

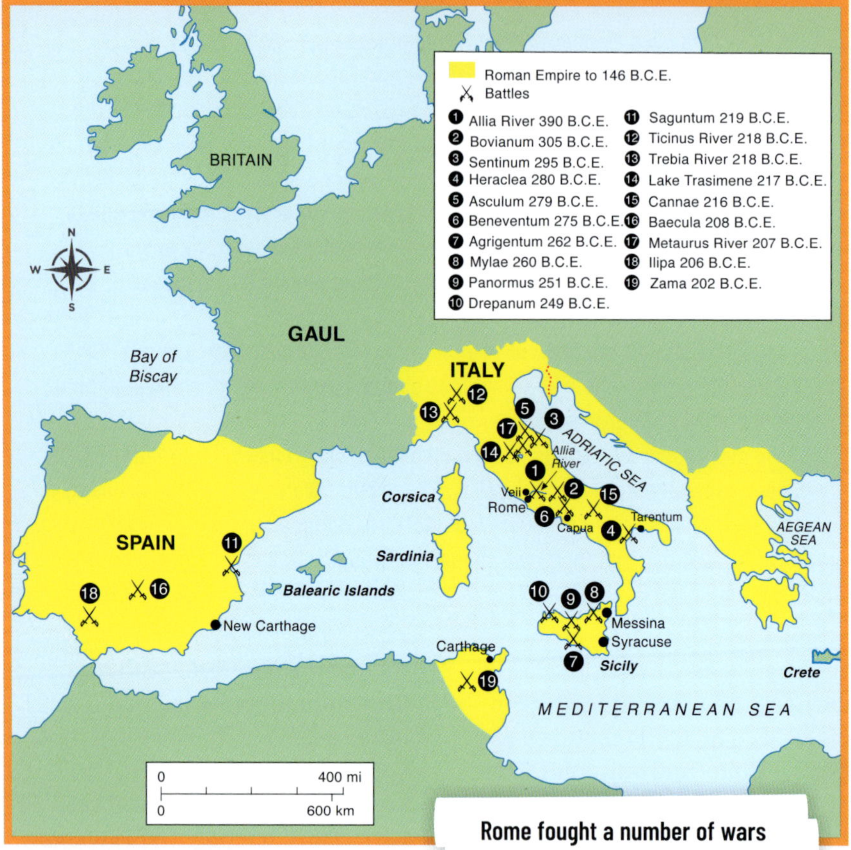

Rome fought a number of wars to become the dominant power in Italy and slowly expanded around the Mediterranean.

was supreme in Italy. Its power rested on a system of alliances with cities throughout Italy and the colonies of citizen settlers it established at strategic points.

The Greek cities of southern Italy watched Roman expansion with increasing alarm. In 281 BCE one of them invited Pyrrhus, the king of Epirus in western Greece, to help them fight Rome. Pyrrhus brought his army of 20,000 across the Adriatic Sea. His army included 20 elephants, the first time the Romans had met these animals in war. He fought two major battles against the Romans, at Heraclea in 280 BCE and at Asculum in 279 BCE. Although Pyrrhus won both battles, his losses were very heavy (4,000 men out of 11,000 at Heraclea), giving rise to the expression “Pyrrhic victory.” The term is still used today to describe a battle in which the victor’s losses are so heavy that very little military advantage is gained. In 275 BCE the Romans finally defeated Pyrrhus at the Battle of Beneventum and he left Italy.

Rome's expansion southward now brought it to the Strait of Messina, which separates Italy from the island of Sicily. Sicily had, since the beginning of the fifth century BCE, been the site of a war between Carthage, a North African city that had colonized the western half of the island, and Syracuse, a Greek city. In 264 BCE Rome, Syracuse, and Carthage became involved in a dispute over the city of Messina. This dispute turned into a war between the Carthaginians and the Romans, known as the First Punic War. (Punic was the name the Romans called the Carthaginians.)

Rome Gains Sicily

Sicily was the first battlefield of the war. A Roman army besieged Agrigentum, a Carthaginian stronghold on the island, in 262 BCE. The Romans defeated a Carthaginian army that was sent to help. Although the Carthaginian defenders of Agrigentum escaped, the Romans had gained control of most of Sicily.

The war shifted to the sea. The Carthaginians had an excellent navy while the Romans had no tradition of fighting at sea. The Romans recognized their shortcomings and developed a clever device that would allow them to destroy the Carthaginian advantage. It was called the corvus or "raven" and consisted of a plank with a spike

A Roman warship uses its corvus or "raven" to attach itself to an enemy vessel so that Roman infantry can use their superior skills in close-quarters fighting to win a victory against better sailors.

HANNIBAL BARCA

Hannibal was born into a Carthaginian military family, the Barca, in 247 BCE. His father, Hamilcar, had been an important commander in Sicily during the First Punic War. When Hamilcar went to Spain in 237 BCE he took Hannibal with him, after making him swear an oath always to be hostile to Rome.

Hannibal lived up to the oath he swore. His successes on the battlefield against the Roman army at the Trebia River in 218 BCE, at Lake Trasimene in 217 BCE, and most famously at Cannae in 216 BCE remain some of the greatest victories of all time.

Hannibal's genius for war rivaled that of Alexander the Great. He was as brave as Alexander, although he took fewer risks on the battlefield. He shared the hardships of his soldiers and thereby earned their loyalty. His one mistake was the maneuver that made him famous. By crossing the Alps into Italy, he made it almost impossible for his army to receive reinforcements. After his defeat at the Battle of Zama in 202 BCE Hannibal became a hunted man. He committed suicide rather than surrender in 183 BCE.

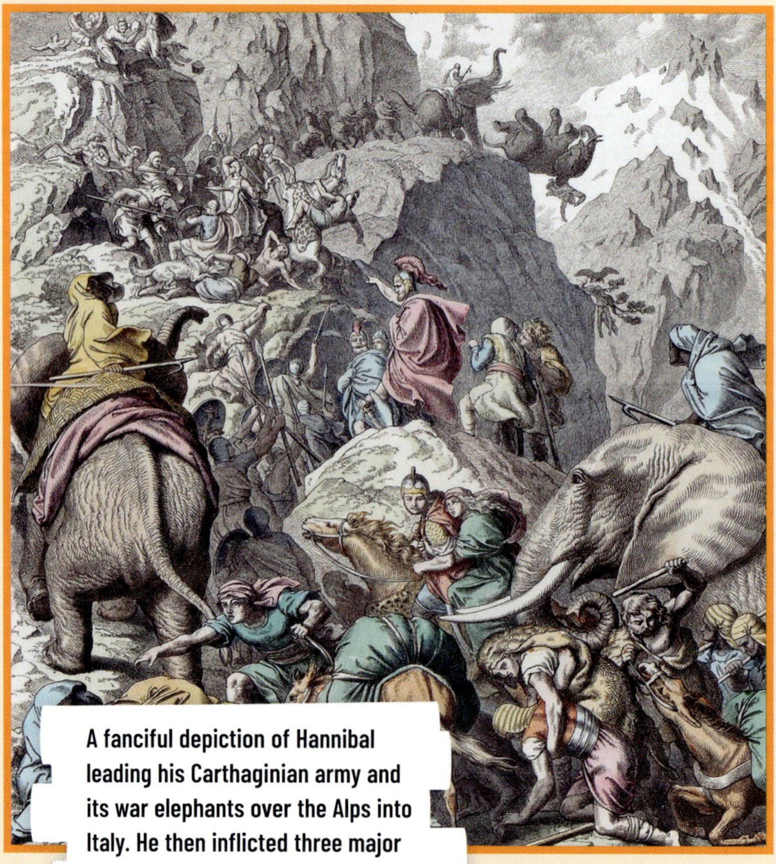

A fanciful depiction of Hannibal leading his Carthaginian army and its war elephants over the Alps into Italy. He then inflicted three major defeats on the Roman legions.

at the top positioned at the front of a warship. When an enemy ship came close, the plank was dropped onto it, and the spike ensured it could not escape. Then Roman soldiers could run across the plank and fight it out on the enemy ship. At the Battle of Mylae in 260 BCE the device enabled the Romans to win a great naval victory.

War with Carthage

In 256 BCE the Roman Senate decided to strike directly against Carthaginian territory in North Africa. They brought together a large fleet of warships but the Carthaginians had been able to build a slightly larger one in the years since their defeat at Mylae. The two rival fleets met off the the south coast of Sicily. Again the Romans won because the Carthaginians did not manage to carry out their complex plan for dealing with the raven by attacking Roman ships from the stern.

The Romans now landed a large army in North Africa, commanded by Marcus Atilius Regulus. Regulus defeated the first Carthaginian army sent against him and they almost began peace talks. But in 255 BCE a Spartan mercenary general named Xanthippus arrived in Carthage. He reorganized the Carthaginian army and destroyed Regulus's army at the Battle of Tunes. The Roman fleet suffered heavy losses in a storm. More than 280 ships were sunk and close to 100,000 soldiers were lost. These disasters for Roman forces encouraged Carthage to renew its war effort.

Continued Carthaginian Campaign

The remainder of the war was fought in Sicily. The Romans defeated a Carthaginian army at the Battle of Panormus in 251 BCE but suffered a major naval defeat at Drepanum in 249 BCE. The Romans lost nearly 100 ships; the Carthaginians none. Five years of stalemate only ended in 242 BCE when the Romans seized the Carthaginian bases at Drepanum and Lilybaeum in Sicily. The Romans then defeated the Carthaginian fleet in 241 BCE and Carthage gave up. All of Sicily was surrendered to Rome.

Between 241 and 219 BCE the Romans seized the island of Sardinia, while the Carthaginians created a new empire in Spain. This new empire caused the Second Punic War. The Romans had allied with the city of Saguntum in northeast Spain to block the Carthaginian expansion. The commander of the Carthaginians in Spain, Hannibal, captured Saguntum in 219 BCE. Rome then declared war.

Slaughter at the Trebia River

Hannibal recognized that Rome's great strength lay in its control of Italy and its large population. He decided to invade Italy by leading his army overland from Spain, through southern France, and across the Alps into Italy. Hannibal began his march early in 218 BCE, and arrived in Italy that fall. Before winter put a stop to the fighting Hannibal fought two battles against the Romans in Italy. At the Ticinus River he defeated a smaller Roman army and at the Trebia River he defeated a larger one.

Hannibal ambushed the next Roman army sent against him in the spring of 217 BCE as it marched along Lake Trasimene in central Italy. Hannibal killed or captured three-quarters of its 40,000 soldiers. He now marched into southern Italy. He hoped to encourage the cities of Italy to break their alliance with Rome. The Romans used a similar strategy. They sent an army to Spain to conquer the Carthaginians there.

Hannibal's Greatest Victory

The Romans now organized the biggest army in their history, some 75,000 soldiers, and sent it against Hannibal. At Cannae, in 216 BCE, Hannibal destroyed the army. He had won his greatest victory, but gained little. The determination of the Romans to continue the war caused them to bring every Roman man into the army, including slaves and convicts.

Hannibal learned that Roman garrisons in many of the cities of southern Italy prevented them joining him in his war against Rome. Especially worrying was his failure to control a port. Hannibal tried hard to capture Tarentum, a major port in the south of Italy. He did not succeeded until 213 BCE.

By this time all the advantages gained at Cannae had been lost. In 215 BCE a Roman army had won

In 216 BCE a newly raised Roman army was defeated at the Battle of Cannae by Hannibal. Here the Roman consul Lucius Aemilius Paullus is told of the scale of the defeat and chooses to remain and die with his men.

THE REPUBLICAN LEGION

The Roman republican legion consisted of four types of infantry. The velites were young men taught to fight as light infantry. The hastati were slightly older and more experienced. The principes were veterans of around 30 years of age. The triarii were the oldest soldiers.

These groups were organized into maniples, or subdivisions, of between 120 and 160 men, except for the triarii, who were organized in groups of 60 to 80. Above the maniple was the cohort. This larger unit consisted of 120 to 160 each of velites, hastati, and principes, 60 to 80 triarii, and a cavalry turma (unit) of 30 men. A standard Roman legion, with a strength of around 4,500 to 5,000 troops, consisted of 10 such cohorts. The legion proved a flexible, fast-moving unit. The maniples were placed in a checkerboard formation, allowing them to maneuver over rough ground.

Legionaries carried a variety of weapons. The hastati and principes carried 7-foot (2.1-m) javelins, which were thrown at close range. The javelin, known as a pilum, had a head of soft metal with a slender neck, which tended to bend when it struck a target and so could not be reused by an enemy. The triarii carried a 12-foot (3.6-m) spear. All of these troops also used a short sword—the gladius—which was thrust rather than used as a slashing weapon. The velites carried javelins and darts. Extra firepower was provided by slingers and bowmen.

a victory in Spain over Hannibal's brother, Hasdrubal. However, instead of reinforcing Hannibal, the Carthaginian Council chose to send troops to Spain. Political conflict in the important Sicilian city of Syracuse had brought a pro-Carthaginian faction to power but the Romans had sent an army to the island to besiege the city. The Carthaginians did not have the military resources to support Hannibal in Italy as well as Syracuse in Sicily and Hasdrubal in Spain.

Hannibal Marches on Rome

In 211 BCE Hannibal marched to the outskirts of Rome. Symbolically it showed the world that the Romans could do nothing to stop him. In fact it was an indication that, while he was winning battles, he was losing the war. The Romans refused to fight him. Instead they attacked those cities that had joined his alliance. Hannibal had hoped the Romans would abandon the siege of Capua, his most important ally, if he advanced on Rome. However, the Romans left enough troops to maintain the siege and recaptured Capua later that year. They also captured Syracuse. By the following year Hannibal had been isolated and cut off from Carthage.

In 210 BCE the Senate sent Publius Cornelius Scipio to command the Roman forces in Spain. He captured New Carthage on the coast of eastern Spain in 209 BCE. He then defeated Hasdrubal's army at Baecula the next year.

THE BATTLE OF CANNAE

The Battle of Cannae in 216 BCE was Hannibal's greatest victory and has served as a model for generals throughout history. Hannibal's advance through Italy had brought him to Apulia, where he met a Roman army determined to fight. The Romans had 75,000 soldiers, Hannibal 40,000.

The Roman commander, Gaius Terentius Varro, had studied Hannibal's previous battles. He aimed to break through the Carthaginian center, and to do so fast enough to avoid being encircled. Varro reinforced the center of the army in the hope of breaking through more quickly.

Hannibal reinforced his own center once he saw the Roman attacking formation. He also arranged it in an outward-facing crescent, so that the flanks of the Roman formation would turn inward as they attacked the Carthaginian army. They could then be attacked more easily from the flanks.

Hannibal's center held off the Romans long enough for Carthaginian cavalry and infantry on the flanks to encircle the legions. The Carthaginians killed about 60,000 Romans. Hannibal lost about 6,000 soldiers.

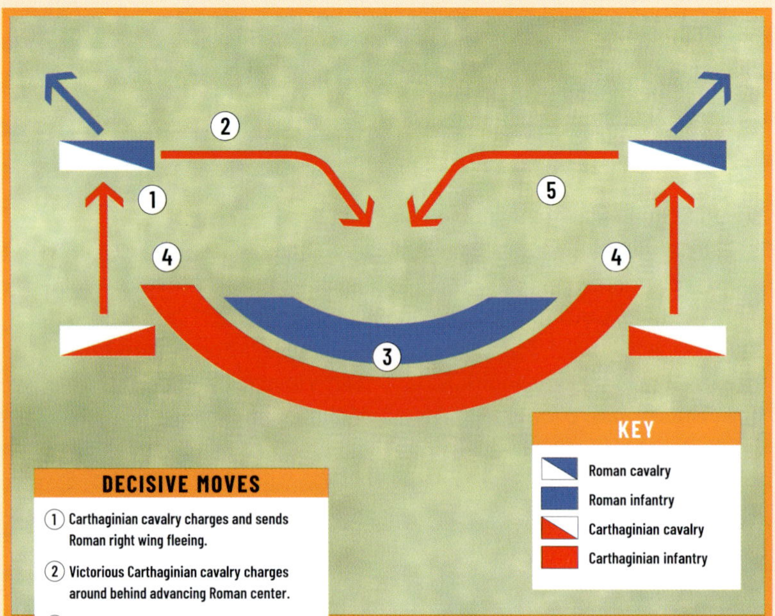

DECISIVE MOVES

1. Carthaginian cavalry charges and sends Roman right wing fleeing.
2. Victorious Carthaginian cavalry charges around behind advancing Roman center.
3. The Carthaginian center halts Roman attack.
4. Carthaginian infantry advances against both flanks of stalled Roman attack.
5. After driving off enemy cavalry, the Carthaginian right flank swings around to complete the destruction of the Roman Army. The Roman legions are surrounded and slaughtered.

The Battle of Cannae was Hannibal's finest victory. He enticed the Romans into attacking his center and then surrounded them. Caught in a trap, the Roman legions were annihilated.

The Battle of Zama, 202 BCE. Hannibal deployed elephants against the Romans but Roman commander Scipio devised tactics that made them unable to break the Roman line.

Hasdrubal knew that Hannibal's army in Italy would not survive for long without reinforcements. He decided after the Battle of Baecula to take what was left of his army to Italy. He arrived in 207 BCE and marched south to meet Hannibal. The Romans, however, learned of Hasdrubal's plans. This enabled them to intercept Hasdrubal's army at the Battle of the Metaurus River. Hasdrubal died along with 10,000 of his troops.

Sold into Slavery

In 206 BCE Scipio defeated the Carthaginians in Spain at Ilipa. Spain was now in Roman hands. Hasdrubal's defeat and the Battle of Ilipa sealed the fate of Hannibal's army. In 204 BCE Scipio invaded North Africa. Hannibal and Scipio met at Zama in 202 BCE Scipio's superiority in cavalry enabled him to defeat the Carthaginians. Hannibal fled but was pursued by the Romans for the rest of his life. The treaty ending the war reduced Carthage to a small city-state.

Carthage and Rome went to war again in 149 BCE. This time Carthage was captured in 146 BCE. Survivors of the siege were sold into slavery and the city was razed to the ground.

Rome: From Republic to Empire

Rome's victory over Carthage in the Second Punic War made it the leading power in the central Mediterranean. It had conquered Sicily and was preeminent in Spain. Now Rome turned its attention east, to Greece. Greece was part of a wider Greek culture that had dominated the Middle East since the conquests of Alexander the Great. Many of these kingdoms were ruled by experienced generals. This did not put Rome off, however. In 200 BCE Rome attacked King Philip V of Macedonia.

The Romans landed an army of two legions on the west coast of Greece. Philip V promptly marched his army from the Hellespont to Greece and stopped the Romans from getting any farther than Illyria, a mountainous region to the northwest of Macedonia.

The Roman Senate now appointed a new commander, Titus Quinctius Flamininus. He achieved the victory that earlier Roman leaders could not. At the Battle of Cynoscephalae in 197 BCE he destroyed Philip's army. Some 13,000 Greeks were killed. Rome declared Greece to be under its protection.

A bust of Hannibal Barca, implacable foe of Rome. He committed suicide 183 BCE rather than surrender to the Romans.

THE BATTLE OF CYNOSCEPHALAE

The Battle of Cynoscephalae in 197 BCE highlighted the different strengths of the Roman and Macedonian military systems. Three days before the battle the Macedonian army of Philip V and the Roman legions of Titus Quinctius Flamininus had lost contact with one another. Coincidentally, both armies started marching toward the same city. In a range of hills their advance guards met on a foggy morning and began fighting.

When both generals learned of this, each deployed his army for battle. Philip's soldiers had the advantage of starting from higher ground. His phalanx formed in two huge blocks. He led the one on the right in a charge on one of the Roman legions and pushed it back. The other half, however, did not form up before the other Roman legion, led by Flamininus, charged.

As the second phalanx began to retreat an alert tribune (officer) in the rear ranks of Flamininus's army led a small force against the rear of Philip's first phalanx. This disordered it and allowed the first Roman legion to recover and attack. Philip saw that the battle was over and retreated. The Roman legion had beaten the hitherto invincible Macedonian phalanx.

Lack of Reward

One of Rome's Greek allies against Philip, the Confederacy of Aetolia, did not believe it had received sufficient reward for its support. The Confederacy turned to the Seleucid emperor, Antiochus III, and invited him to free Greece from Rome. In 192 BCE Antiochus landed in Greece with an army of 10,000. The Romans also landed an army in Greece led by Marcus Acilius Glabrio. Antiochus led his army to the pass at Thermopylae, planning to defend it as the Spartans had done against the Persians in 480 BCE. The Romans outflanked Antiochus's army by following the route the Persians had taken. Antiochus fled back to Asia Minor.

The war then shifted from Greece to the west coast of Asia Minor. The island of Rhodes and the kingdom of Pergamum both joined Rome against Antiochus. The fleet of Rhodes was a valuable addition to the Roman forces. The Roman and Rhodian fleet defeated Antiochus's navy twice during 190 BCE.

Antiochus's fleet at the first battle, at Side on the south coast of Asia Minor, included a squadron commanded by Hannibal, the Carthaginian general, who had found asylum with the emperor.

Death of Hannibal

The Romans had elected Lucius Cornelius Scipio, whose brother Publius had defeated Hannibal at the Battle of Zama in 202 BCE, to command the army. This allowed Lucius to select Publius as one of his officers, to make sure he had the best possible advice. Lucius crossed into Asia Minor and fought Antiochus's army at Magnesia. Antiochus attempted to copy

Alexander the Great by leading his cavalry in a flank attack. But he failed to implement Alexander's tactics and left his phalanx unsupported. The Romans were able to force the phalanx into a hollow square. Then they caused Antiochus's elephants to panic and run into the square. The Roman legionaries charged and won a complete victory. Asia Minor, what is now Turkey, was at their mercy.

Under the terms of the peace Antiochus lost all his empire in western Asia Minor. He was also required to surrender Hannibal. The Carthaginian managed to get away to Bithynia, a country on the north coast of Asia Minor. However, in 183 BCE Rome mediated to end a war between Bithynia and Rome's ally in the eastern Mediterranean, Pergamum. Rome demanded that the king of Bithynia surrender Hannibal as one of the peace terms. The great Carthaginian general, probably the finest commander of the age, committed suicide rather than surrender.

Philip spent the years after his defeat by Rome rebuilding Macedonia's power. After his death in 179 BCE his son, Perseus, continued his father's policy but avoided doing anything that would antagonise the Romans. While Perseus may have had no wish to fight Rome, the king of Pergamum, Eumenes II, wanted Rome to fight Perseus. Eumenes accused Perseus of wanting war. The Romans eventually believed him. In 172 BCE the Roman Senate once again declared war on Macedonia.

The surrender of Perseus after the Battle of Pydna in 168 BCE. This was the end of the once powerful Macedonian state, its army completely defeated.

ROMAN FORTIFICATIONS AND SIEGE WARFARE

The ordinary Roman soldier carried a huge weight of equipment on a forked stick over his shoulder. Part of this heavy load included tools for digging earthworks for sieges and the fortified camps they were ordered to prepare each night.

Sieges featured frequently in Roman warfare but the principles were no different from those used by the Assyrians several centuries before. The first step was to dig trenches around the place under siege. At Alesia, during Julius Caesar's wars in Gaul, two sets were built, one facing the town and the other facing outward to defend against a relieving force. The objective was to prevent supplies from reaching the besieged army. At Athens in 86 BCE the defending army was reduced to boiling leather for food.

For the assault a huge ramp, such as visitors can still see at Masada, now in Israel, might be built to get siege towers to the walls. If the Roman attack succeeded, civilians would be slaughtered or sold into slavery. Any treasure would be looted and carried back to Rome.

The Phalanx's Last Battle

Perseus's army defeated two Roman ones attempting to invade Macedonia in 171 and 170 BCE. The Senate then sent Lucius Aemilius Paullus to Greece. Paullus restored the morale of the Roman army and advanced to battle. In 168 BCE, at the Battle of Pydna, the Macedonian phalanx went into battle for what turned out to be the last time.

Its left wing fell into disorder while advancing over rough terrain. The Romans counterattacked the disorganized phalanx. The Macedonian advance turned into a disorderly retreat. Some 30,000 Macedonian soldiers were killed or captured. Perseus was taken prisoner. The kingdom of Macedonia ceased to exist.

While Rome fought in Greece, the Seleucid Empire had invaded Egypt. The Seleucid army virtually controlled the whole country when Rome sent an ambassador to impose a peace settlement. The ambassador, Popillius Laenas, met the Seleucid emperor, Antiochus IV, at Alexandria. Laenas handed the emperor a document ordering him to leave Egypt. Antiochus asked for time to think about this. Laenas, using his cane, drew a circle around Antiochus and said: "Answer yes or no before you leave the circle." Antiochus knew he could not defeat Rome, and said "yes." This incident showed Rome's mastery of the eastern Mediterranean.

Rebellion Against Rome

When Antiochus withdrew from Egypt, he marched to his province of Palestine. He was short of money and knew that the Jewish temple at Jerusalem contained a large treasure. The Jewish people naturally objected to Antiochus taking this away. Antiochus decided

Jugurtha, the Numidian king, is brought before the Roman commander, Lucius Cornelius Sulla, in chains after being betrayed. Sulla was one of a number of Roman commanders who would wrestle for power.

to abolish their religion. The Jewish people, who had suffered foreign rule for 500 years, rebelled. A 20-year guerrilla war ensued, ending in the creation of an independent state of Israel in 143 BCE.

About the time of Israel's independence Rome's own lengthy guerrilla conflict was coming to an end. After the Carthaginians had been defeated in Spain in 206 BCE, the Roman Senate placed a permanent garrison of two legions there. The tribal states of the Iberian peninsula had no wish to exchange Carthaginian rule for Roman rule. For over 50 years the Romans faced rebellions, which they punished with massacres of thousands of Spanish tribespeople.

THE FOUNDATION OF THE ROMAN EMPIRE

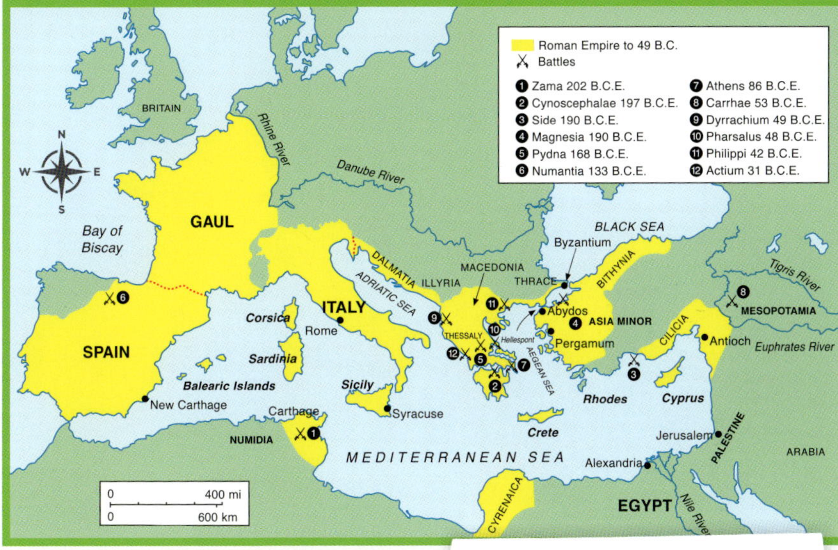

Through wars and alliances Roman influence spread across the whole Mediterranean world in the final years of the republic and laid the foundations for the Roman Empire.

No ordinary Roman soldier wanted to fight in Spain. There was little of value to plunder, and the chances of a legionary being killed or badly wounded in a small skirmish were high. For senior commanders, however, there was the opportunity to gain renown by winning a war.

In 149 BCE the Spanish tribes in the far west, called the Lusitanians and the Celtiberians, rebelled after the Romans had killed their chiefs and their bodyguards. Virathus, a Lusitanian who had commanded troops in the Roman army, was the leader of the revolt.

For 10 years Virathus defended Lusitania against the Romans until he was killed by a traitor and the revolt collapsed. Two years later the Celtiberians rebelled again. They established a capital at Numantia in northeastern Spain, which the Romans sent an army to besiege. In 133 BCE Numantia fell and was totally destroyed.

A Century of War

Rome was constantly at war during the next century. The Italian city imposed its direct rule over many single states or tribal areas that had a Mediterranean seacoast. The first conflicts led to a reform of the Roman army. A war against Numidia, a country in North Africa, dragged on and on as the Numidian king, Jugurtha, used guerrilla tactics that avoided battles.

Roman soldiers, except in times of national emergency, normally paid for their own equipment, attracted by the prospect of plunder and grants of land. But the North Africans, like the Spanish tribes, were not wealthy. In order to attract

A representation of Gaius Marius on a coin. Marius reformed the legions. He made his soldiers carry heavy loads. They called themselves "Marius' mules."

volunteers, the Roman Senate agreed to pay for the soldiers' equipment. The poorest Roman citizens could now afford to join the army, with the prospect of a grant of land at the end of the war as an added incentive. The Roman army was slowly being changed into a fully-professional fighting machine, one that was paid for and maintained by the empire's vast and increasing wealth.

This measure provided enough volunteers to fight Jugurtha. An imaginative commander, Gaius Marius, won the war in 106 BCE. He placed garrisons throughout Numidia, denying the North Africans bases for their guerrillas. Jugurtha was betrayed to the Romans and made a prisoner.

Ambitious Generals

Jugurtha surrendered to a young officer in Marius's army named Lucius Cornelius Sulla. After Sulla returned to Italy, he took part in a war to restore Roman rule over a number of its allies who had rebelled. Afterward Sulla took an army to the eastern Mediterranean

GAIUS JULIUS CAESAR

Gaius Julius Caesar's family was part of the Roman nobility. He served in the Roman legions stationed in Greece and Turkey from 82 to 74 BCE before receiving his first independent command in Spain.

His successes helped him to win election as one of the two Roman consuls, or presidents, in 60 BCE. Afterward he was given a five-year (later extended to ten) command of Roman armies in Gaul. His conquests added Gaul to the empire.

Caesar was not a brilliant commander like Alexander the Great or Hannibal. He was a good general in an era of very ordinary officers. But he was a poor organizer. More than once he was rescued from disasters of his own making by the determination of his soldiers to achieve victory. Caesar could always count on the loyalty of his legionaries. He also benefited from the bad decisions made by his opponents on several occasions.

A bust of Julius Caesar. Until his assassination in 44 BCE Caesar was the most prominent of the generals who tried to take power in the last days of the Roman republic. His nephew Augustus later became the first emperor of Rome.

where Mithridates, king of Pontus, a country on the Black Sea coast, had invaded the Roman-controlled part of the Aegean coast and then Greece. Sulla defeated Mithridates' army at Athens in 86 BCE. When Sulla crossed into Asia, Mithridates negotiated a peace in 84 BCE.

Sulla agreed to a compromise settlement because civil war had

THE IMPERIAL LEGION

Gaius Marius reorganized the Roman army at the end of the second century BCE. He established the pattern that was used by the army for 400 years. Marius abolished the maniples. They were replaced with cohorts, nine of 480 soldiers and one of 800. He also made the heavy throwing javelin, the pilum, the standard weapon for all the soldiers. All soldiers were now infantry, armored with chain-mail corselets, and carrying shields and short swords. In Marius's time legionaries served a 6-year enlistment but this was later extended to 16.

The army recruited its light infantry and cavalry from its non-Italian allies such as the Numidians of North Africa, Gauls, and Germans. During the first century BCE these auxiliary troops only served for the duration of a single campaign. However, they later enlisted for a fixed term of service, 16 years like the legionaries, and were organized into permanent units.

broken out in Rome between rivals in the Senate. It was the first in a series of wars that was to change Rome from a republic to a monarchy. Sulla defeated his rival generals in 82 BCE and established a dictatorship that also murdered many on the losing side.

Sulla gave up his dictatorship in 79 BCE. His example of the successful military leader who intervened in politics became the model all Roman politicians copied. Another war against Mithridates between 75 and 65 BCE helped establish the reputation of Gnaeus Pompeius, an ambitious Roman officer, even though all the battles had been won by another general.

In 59 BCE three successful generals, Pompeius, Marcus Licinius Crassus, and Gaius Julius Caesar, effectively took control of the Roman Senate. The Senate gave each of them control of the military forces in a part of the Roman Empire. Two of them, Crassus in the Middle East and Caesar in Gaul (modern France), started wars to expand the empire. Crassus's expedition against the Parthian kingdom of Mesopotamia ended in defeat at Carrhae in 53 BCE, but Caesar's campaigns in Gaul added it to the empire. Caesar even managed to land in Britain in 55 and 54 BCE, although he did not stay for long on either occasion.

The death of Licinius Crassus at Carrhae left Pompeius and Julius Caesar rivals for supreme power at Rome. This rivalry turned into a civil war in 49 BCE. Pompeius withdrew from Italy (with most of the members of the Senate) to assemble an army in Greece. Julius Caesar first invaded Spain, where a large army loyal to Pompeius had to be defeated. He then crossed the Adriatic to land at Dyrrachium in western Greece.

After capturing this port, he advanced into Thessaly and defeated Pompeius at the Battle of Pharsalus in 48 BCE. Pompeius fled to Egypt, where he was murdered.

The Battle of Actium was fought by Octavian against Cleopatra and Antonius in 31 BCE. It involved more than 800 ships but was decided when part of Antonius's fleet retreated or surrendered. Octavian's victory paved the way for him to become the first Roman emperor.

Julius Caesar followed. He found Egypt close to civil war between Ptolemy XII and Cleopatra, brother and sister. Julius Caesar backed Cleopatra. In 45 BCE, after victories in North Africa and Spain over the remaining armies of Pompeius's supporters, Julius Caesar returned to Rome. In 44 BCE he was assassinated by nobles fearful of his power.

Another civil war began. Caesar's assassins fled to Greece, where they raised an army. They were followed by Marcus Antonius, Caesar's second-in-command, and Caesar's nephew, Octavian. At Philippi in 42 BCE the assassins were defeated. Octavian and Antonius split the empire, Octavian taking the west and Antonius the east. Antonius made an alliance with Cleopatra.

For 10 years Octavian and Antonius shared power. But in 32 BCE Octavian persuaded the Senate to declare war on Egypt. Antonius brought a fleet to the west coast of Greece. Octavian's fleet defeated Antonius and Cleopatra at Actium in 31 BCE.

Cleopatra and Antonius committed suicide. Octavian became ruler of the Roman world, taking the title Augustus. Rome had an emperor.

The Enemies of Imperial Rome

In 27 BCE Julius Caesar's nephew Octavian emerged as the victor from a long series of civil wars. Although he was careful to respect the traditional forms of republican government Octavian was effectively sole ruler. For the next 450 years Rome was an empire largely ruled by a single individual. Octavian renamed himself Augustus and set about restoring stability for the Roman world. This led him to wage wars across the existing frontiers. The Roman Empire began to grow rapidly.

Before the reign of this first emperor much of the Roman Empire had been acquired almost accidentally, after a victorious military campaign. Augustus, however, conquered territory to give his empire stable frontiers that would be easy to defend from attack.

These frontiers frequently coincided with rivers or mountain ranges. Augustus first visited Gaul and set up a number of military camps along the Rhine River and near important passes through the Alps. He then went to Spain to impose Roman rule on the warlike tribes of the country's northwest region.

An illustration depicting the destruction of three Roman legions by German tribesmen in 9 CE.

Changing Plans

After the Spanish wars ended in 19 BCE, Augustus embarked on a new phase of expansion. He aimed to create a river frontier from the North Sea to the Black Sea, at first following the courses of the Rhine and Danube rivers. Between 29 and 27 BCE a Roman army had occupied the land north of Macedonia, modern Serbia. Ten years later Augustus sent his adopted son, Tiberius Caesar Augustus, and Tiberius's brother, Nero Claudius Drusus, to conquer the area that is now Austria. An invasion of Gaul in 16 BCE by the German Sagambri tribe made Augustus alter his plans. Instead of the Rhine, he decided to push the Roman border even farther east to the Weser River.

Roman troops now advanced far into Germany. Some legionaries in the north even reached the Elbe, a river to the east of the Weser. In the south the army crossed the Danube to impose Roman rule on the Bohemian plain. By 5 CE the Romans felt confident enough to send a fleet through the North Sea to the mouth of the Elbe to meet the advancing legions.

Octavian became the first Roman emperor in 27 BCE and began an era that saw the Roman Empire stabilize its borders throughout Europe and the Mediterranean.

THE LIMES

The limes, from a Latin word used for roads marking boundaries between farms or orchards, provided a barrier that kept barbarians out of the Roman Empire. They also gave a Roman army crossing the frontier a protected base for its supplies and a refuge in case it had to retreat after a defeat. The structure of the limes varied depending on the frontier defended.

In Britain it took the permanent form of Hadrian's impressive stone wall dividing north and south. Along the Rhine River a wall of upright logs and an earthen rampart connected legionary and auxiliary camps. Here the barbarians lacked the technology to overcome fortifications.

In arid North Africa, where there were desert raiders, and the Middle East, where the Parthians and Sassanid Persians challenged Rome, the Romans preferred a network of legionary forts and fortified towns. In each area the Romans kept possible enemies or raiders out of the geographical area with methods appropriate to the technology of their opponents.

Part of Hadrian's Wall in Britain. Roman limes were either complex structures or more basic constructions. Their style was often dictated by the natural terrain and the knowledge of the enemies that might threaten a frontier.

However, a revolt by German tribes in Bohemia in 6 CE showed how fragile the Roman gains were. It took three years of hard fighting in central Europe to restore Roman authority. Augustus had to deploy the largest field army seen since the civil wars.

"Give Me Back My Legions"

No sooner had Bohemia been reconquered than a major disaster struck the Romans. The massacre, almost to a man, of three legions marching through the dense, almost impassable, Teutoberg Forest in northern Germany in 9 CE shattered the dream of a Weser River frontier. Those Roman soldiers the Germans captured became human sacrifices to the German gods. Six years later a Roman army found the bones of their 15,000 comrades. For the rest of his life Augustus was often reduced to tears by the memory, demanding of his long-dead defeated general, "Varus, give me back my legions."

The hard fighting in Bohemia and the catastrophe of the Teutoberg Forest were factors in causing a mutiny in the army following Augustus's death in 14 CE. Tiberius, his successor, used this unrest and the difficulty of finding new recruits to put a brake on further Roman advances in northern Europe. The last act of expansion in this region was an invasion of Britain in 43 CE by Emperor Claudius. The conquest of Britain illustrated the problems the Romans faced on the frontiers. Various attempts to conquer the whole island failed and the northern frontier was finally stabilized along the line of Hadrian's Wall in what is now northern England.

The Eastern Frontier

The defeat of a Roman army at the Battle of Carrhae, Mesopotamia, in 53 BCE by the kingdom of Parthia had been a factor in turning Augustus's attention northward to lands that could be conquered more easily. Carrhae, and an unprofitable campaign by a Roman army between 36 and 34 BCE, led to a negotiated settlement between the two in 20 BCE which supposedly set the boundary between Parthia and the Roman Empire for all time.

Tiberius continued Augustus's peace policy toward Parthia by refusing to take advantage of a Parthian civil war to expand eastward. Tiberius made a new agreement in 18 CE with the victor of the civil war that confirmed the earlier one. However, Parthia broke the treaty in 35 CE, launching the first of two wars against Armenia, an ally of Rome. Rome defeated Parthia in both wars.

Rome's Political Upheavals

The new Roman emperor Nero was envious of the popularity gained by the victorious general Gnaeus Domitius Corbulo in the second war. Nero charged Corbulo with treason and ordered him to commit suicide. Besides depriving Rome of a successful military leader, this act also led the empire into civil war. Partly because of this,

ROME'S DACIAN WARS

The barbarian Dacians lived north of the Danube River in the area of what is now Romania. During the first century CE they began to develop a more civilized way of life, including building fortified towns. In 89 CE the Dacian ruler, Decebalus, sided with two other German tribes that the Romans had attacked. After a military defeat the Roman emperor, Domitian, had to sign a harsh treaty that Decebalus helped negotiate. In 101 CE Emperor Trajan sought revenge by provoking a war with Decebalus. The conflict lasted two years. Although the Romans won several bloody battles, they did not gain a decisive advantage. The two sides agreed to a truce. The war resumed in 105 CE. Afterward Trajan erected a column in Rome decorated with scenes from the campaign. It shows how the Roman army crossed the Danube using a bridge of boats, the advance on the enemy capital, the defeat of the Dacians outside it, and the suicide of Decebalus. His head was brought to Rome and ritually displayed there.

the Senate declared Nero a public enemy. Emperor Nero committed suicide but there was no one to take his place. During 69 CE four different men claimed to be the Roman emperor. Different parts of the army supported different candidates. Several battles were fought in northern Italy before Vespasian emerged the winner. During his reign two rebellions, one by the Jews in Palestine and the other in northeastern Gaul and Germany, had to be defeated. But in comparison with previous centuries, the empire enjoyed an age of unusual peace and security. Major wars were fought only on the periphery of the empire, and barely affected the daily life of the majority of the empire's population.

Trajan's Wars of Conquest

In Europe, on the edges of the empire, new kingdoms emerged. One of these, that of the Dacians in the area of what is now Romania, was sufficiently powerful locally to defeat a Roman invasion in 85 CE. A second Roman attempt between 101 and 107 CE, led by the emperor Trajan, conquered the Dacians. Trajan also extended the empire eastward. He added a new province called Mesopotamia to the empire after a successful war against the Parthians. This extended the empire to its greatest ever extent.

Defeating the Germans

During the final 40 years of peace and stabilty in the second century CE there were some indications of the problems that were to follow in the third century. Alarmingly, in 168 CE an alliance of German tribes—the Marcomanni, the Langobardi, and the Quadi—crossed the Danube River. Some of the invaders even reached Aquileia in northern Italy.
The emperor Marcus Aurelius personally took to the field to drive

THE ROMAN EMPIRE

The Roman Empire was at the height of its power during the reigns of the first emperors. They defeated invaders and established strong frontier defenses.

them back across the Danube. At the war's end in 179 CE the Germans had been defeated and the frontier was secure once more.

In 193 CE a new civil war broke out. The ruling emperor Commodus, son of Marcus Aurelius, had been assassinated in 192 CE because of his unpopularity with the Roman Senate. There was no obvious candidate to succeed him. The imperial bodyguard sold the right to the throne to the highest bidder. Different armies put forward their own candidates for the position of emperor.

Late in 193 CE Lucius Septimus Severus, the commander of the Danube frontier, emerged victorious from the war between the three rival claimants for the position of emperor. Severus set about regaining the loyalty of the legions that had supported his opponents during the civil war.

"Enrich the Soldiers"

However, Severus did not find a balance between the interests of army and Senate as Augustus had done. As Severus advised his sons: "Work together, enrich the soldiers, and scorn everyone else."

Severus knew where the true power in the empire lay. The future of the empire was now entirely in the hands of its legions, and the men they promoted to lead it.

The Roman army was about to meet severe challenges. A new set of rulers in Iran, the Sassanid dynasty, had come to power, while more Germanic tribes were putting pressure on the northern frontier. The legions would soon have to fight on several fronts at once.

Sassanid Persia at War

For centuries, the Roman Empire fought wars against the Parthians, a nomadic people who ruled much of Iran. Then, in 224 or 226 CE, Ardashir, the king of Persis, overthrew the Parthians. Their empire passed into his hands. He established a more centralized state and created a new army. The Sassanid Empire was to become one of Rome's most bitter foes. It took advantage of Roman weakness, especially during the third century CE, and even defeated Roman emperors in battle.

Ardashir claimed that he was a descendant of the Persian emperors of the time of Darius and Xerxes. He used this claim to support his demand that Rome give up the eastern provinces of its empire, which had been part of the old Persian Empire. In 230, to make his claim good, Ardashir invaded Mesopotamia, which was then a Roman province. Rome responded slowly to this attack. It took three years to assemble a large army.

There are few known facts about the war that followed. Ardashir at first retreated to Persia but in 241 he renewed his attack. Ardashir died, probably of old age, during this second campaign. He was succeeded by his son, Shapur I.

Shapur captured several important cities before being brought to battle by a Roman army at Resaena in 243. While historians know a battle was fought there in

Shapur I uses the Roman Emperor Valerian as a footstool to help him mount his horse in this 16th-century illustration by Hans Holbein. The capture of Valerian in 260 was a great humiliation for Rome.

THE SASSANID ARMY

Heavily armored horsemen made up the best of the Sassanid army. Their armor covered them from head to foot and sometimes their horses wore armor as well. The Romans called them clibanarii, a word meaning "in an oven" and describing the effect such equipment might have in the hot Middle Eastern summer. Horsemen were armed with 12-foot (3.7-m) spears and their charge usually delivered a decisive blow against the enemy.

On the flanks were swarms of horse-archers. These would ride up to the enemy, firing arrows when they were in range, and then fall back. The archery was intended to disorganize the enemy before the heavy cavalry charged.

Behind the mounted archers the Persians placed elephants imported from India. These were used mostly because their smell upset horses that had never encountered an elephant.

In the rear of the army was a mass of poor-quality infantry armed with spears and shields. They were more useful for digging trenches and building camps than for direct combat.

243, the result of it is not clear. Shapur claimed that he won and that the Romans paid him a sum of money to release the emperor, known as Philip the Arab, from captivity. Little information from the Roman side survives. It is known that Shapur defeated a Roman army at Edessa in 260 and the Emperor Valerian then became his captive.

This war marked the worst Roman setback in the Middle East since the reign of Augustus. Shapur was a very energetic ruler. By the time he died, in either 270 or 273, Roman rule over its Middle Eastern provinces looked fragile. Persia, by contrast, looked strong.

Weak Persian Leadership

The authoritarian regime founded by Ardashir meant that Persian strength was a reflection of the man at the top. However, weaker Persian rulers and political intrigue after Shapur's death allowed Rome to restore its eastern frontier. Between 282 and 283, for example, the Romans reconquered the territory they had given up 40 years before. This was the beginning of a 15-year conflict between Rome and Persia.

At first the advantage in war swung like a clock's pendulum between the two sides. In 294 a new phase began when Narses, a son of Shapur, became Persia's king. He brought much-needed stability to Persia's leadership.

In 296 Narses won a major victory over the Roman army at the Battle of Callinicum, close to Carrhae where the Romans had been defeated by the Parthians in 53 BCE. In 297 a Roman army led by Galerius avenged Callinicum, despite the 25,000 Romans being outnumbered four-to-one.

An Iranian wall relief sculpture of Shapur I being paid homage by two Roman emperors, Philip the Arab and Valerian.

The Persian army was defeated and Narses's family and harem captured. Narses asked for peace talks. The Treaty of Nisibis, ending the war, established a frontier that lasted for 40 years.

Continuing War with Rome

Yet again instability was partly responsible for the length of the peace. Narses died in 302 and his successor, Hormizd II, ruled for only seven years. Shapur II, the heir to Hormizd, was a baby. An Arab king, Thair, showed Persia's weakness to the world when he raided Iran in 320. Shapur was only about 10 years old, but he remembered this insult. Eight years later he took his revenge in the first campaign of his reign. He invaded Arabia and defeated Thair.

Shapur began a new war with Rome in 337. The years since the Treaty of Nisibis seem to have been used by the Persians to construct new fortresses along their border with Rome. Before the war in 337 Romans had easily entered Persian territory but histories of the 337 war are full of accounts of sieges in Persian territory. The Persians had also built siege engines of their own, which they did not have before. This era of siege warfare came to an end in 350, when both Rome and Persia agreed to a truce.

Shapur renewed the war in 358 with an attack on the Roman fortress of Amida. His advance was unexpected and he could have succeeded in reaching the Mediterranean coast had it not been for the garrison of Amida. These brave Roman soldiers withstood a 73-day siege. By the time they surrendered, winter was approaching and Shapur had to stop campaigning for the year.

During the winter the Romans rushed forces to the area and Shapur faced a series of difficult sieges during the following year. By this time a huge Roman army of 65,000 men had been assembled at Antioch, Syria. Shapur chose to

An Iranian metal representation of Shapur II, known as Shapur the Great. He pursued a long series of wars against the Roman Empire.

wait for the Roman attack. In 363 the Roman emperor, Julian, advanced into Mesopotamia. From his writings historians have concluded that Julian aimed to destroy the Persian monarchy.

A Mortal Wound at Night

Shapur shrewdly avoided combat with the Romans. Julian's plan was to march down the Euphrates River to the Persian capital, Ctesiphon, in Mesopotamia, and capture it. But with a Persian army in the area, he could not besiege Ctesiphon without leaving his own forces vulnerable to an attack. Julian chose to bring the Persian army to battle and marched back northward up the Tigris River. During one of the many Persian ambushes Julian was mortally wounded leading a counterattack at night. He might have survived but for the fact that he had not put on his armor.

The new Roman emperor, Jovian, negotiated a peace treaty that left several major fortresses in Persian hands. The Romans agreed to abandon Armenia in the Caucasus. Shapur placed his own candidate on the Armenian throne. The Romans did nothing for 10 years, then supported a rival candidate to the throne. Shapur declared war.

Stalemate with Rome

The Romans had recovered their previous strength along the Syrian–Mesopotamian frontier. They defeated Persian armies twice but could do nothing to break Persian control over Armenia. The stalemate was brought to an end by an invasion of the Roman Empire by barbarian Goths across the Danube River.

The Romans made a peace with Shapur in order to assemble an army to confront the Goths. In 390 Rome and Persia agreed to partition Armenia, which finally brought an end to the wars.

The Fall of Rome

The Roman Empire recovered from a crisis in the third century. However, the enemies of Rome on the frontiers of the empire in the north and in the Middle East were growing stronger. Internal civil wars over the succession of emperors and a decision to split the empire into a western and an eastern half weakened the empire. The western empire was under pressure from barbarian tribes, but the army was often being used by various rivals for power in Rome. Romans were fighting Romans.

Between 217 and 268 the northern border of the empire virtually collapsed. German tribes, pushed up against the frontier by the barbarian tribes farther east, sought some way of settling in the empire. The frontier gave way in three places—the Rhine River, northern Italy, and the Danube River. Franks, a Germanic people, poured across the Rhine in 236. For 20 years they plundered Gaul and Spain until they were defeated.

Italy itself was attacked by a confederacy of German tribes known as the Alemanni. They crossed the Alps every year to raid the fertile valley of the Po River. They found cities that had not

The Vandals attack Rome in 455. The Roman Empress Eudoxia, at the center of the painting, comforts her daughter.

BARBARIAN INVASIONS OF THE LATE ROMAN EMPIRE

The numerous invasions that finally toppled the weakening Roman Empire in the fifth century.

experienced foreign invasion for centuries. For 30 years the Alemanni invaded Italy, until they were defeated by Roman emperor Claudius II at the Battle of Lake Garda in 268.

The most notorious of the German invaders were the Goths. There were two main tribal groups of Goths. The Ostrogoths (East Goths) came from what is now the eastern Ukraine, while the Visigoths (West Goths) came from what is now northeast Romania. When they crossed the Danube in 250 and defeated two Roman armies, they achieved the greatest success of any barbarian tribe up to that time. The Roman emperor Gallus agreed to pay them money if they promised not to raid the empire.

The Goths' greed for plunder caused them to resume the war. They constructed an enormous fleet in the Black Sea. After raiding Roman cities along the coasts of Asia Minor and in the Hellespont, they burst into the Aegean Sea. The Goths spent 15 years sailing from city to city, pillaging as they went. All the great cities of Greece's golden age—Ephesus, Athens, Corinth, Argos, and Sparta—were in turn sacked (destroyed and plundered) by the Gothic pirates.

Threats in the Middle East

The chief threat to Rome lay in the Middle East. The city of Palmyra had been an ally of Rome. In 259 its ruler, Odaenathus, took Rome's side against Sassanid Persia. His defeat of the Persians in 261 was rewarded with a grant of authority over most of Rome's Middle Eastern provinces. While Odaenathus was content with this, others were not. He was murdered and his widow, Zenobia, ruled in his place.

ATTILA THE HUN

Attila became king of the Huns, a nomadic people originating in Central Asia, in 433, after the death of his uncle, Ruas. The Huns had already migrated to the plains north of the Danube River, where they had inflicted a reign of terror on the region's tribes, including the Goths.

The Huns had been allies of the Romans and had received a grant of money from the Romans. In 433, to celebrate Attila's becoming king, this grant was doubled. It was not enough.

Between 441 and 443, and in 447, Attila crossed the Danube into the Balkans. On both occasions he ravaged the area until his grant was increased. In 451 Attila turned west and crossed the Rhine River at the head of 100,000 troops. His plundering was only halted by his defeat at the Battle of Châlons by the Romans and their Gothic allies, who hated the Huns.

Attila sought revenge the next year by invading Italy. However, an outbreak of plague caused him to withdraw. In 453 Attila died of a nosebleed that drowned him in his own blood while he lay drunkenly asleep. His empire rapidly fell apart as his sons fought for control of it.

Attila leads his Huns into Italy. The Huns were not only a direct threat to Rome. They also attacked other peoples and forced them across Rome's frontiers.

In 267 Zenobia declared the independence of Palmyra and also added Egypt to her empire.

When Claudius came to power in 268, Rome was on the verge of collapse, but he reversed the tide of events. In 269 he crushed the Goths at the Battle of Naissus, earning himself the nickname "Gothicus," and looked ready to campaign in the east. Before he had a chance to do this he died of the plague. Fortunately for the empire an equally capable ruler was found to replace him. Emperor Aurelian defeated the Goths in 270, then the Alemanni in 271. Between 272 and 273 he waged fierce war on Palmyra, taking the city and making Zenobia his prisoner. The last of Rome's great emperors, Diocletian, reorganized the empire in 286. It was divided in two—east and west—with two rulers, although Diocletian had authority over them.

Diocletian retired in 305 and civil war broke out between his successors. It ended in 323 when Constantine defeated his last rival at the First Battle of Adrianople. Constantine founded a great new city—Constantinople—to serve as the capital of the whole empire, although he kept Diocletian's reorganization. Constantine died in 337 and civil war broke out again.

The Roman Empire was now in a state of constant war, either among rivals for the throne or with neighboring tribes and kingdoms. Rome was often the target of invasion. The last quarter of the third century saw two military disasters—the Second Battle of Adrianople in 378 and the Battle of the Frigidus River in 394. At Adrianople 40,000 of Rome's best soldiers were killed.

The Sack of Rome

Adrianople was a defeat at the hands of barbarian Goths, while the Frigidus River was part of a civil war between Roman nobles. Casualties among both the Roman troops and the barbarian allies of the victor, Theodosius, were very high. The Roman army never recovered after this defeat. Theodosius's barbarian allies included Visigoths under their king, Alaric. When Alaric felt that he had been poorly rewarded by Theodosius, he sacked Rome in 412.

Alaric leads his Visigothic army into Athens. Alaric was sometimes employed by Roman generals and sometimes fought against them. He demanded large payments for his services and was ruthless in his actions if he was not paid.

By the time the nomadic Huns of Central Asia under Attila first invaded in 441, the Roman empire was close to collapse. Barbarians, from northern and central Europe, chiefly the Burgundians, Lombards, and Vandals, were crossing the Rhine and Danube Rivers into Roman territory. This was due to Rome's weak frontiers and poor leadership. One by one Rome's provinces fell into barbarian hands. When the Ostrogoths deposed the last Roman emperor of the west in 476, the Roman Empire there ended. However, the eastern half of the empire, with its capital at Constantinople, was to survive for nearly 1,000 years.

Ancient China's War Machine

By about the 18th century BCE civilized states emerged in China. As in the Middle East, these states began using warfare to attack other states. The first Chinese armies were entirely foot soldiers. The written records first mention chariots when they describe a battle fought in the last quarter of the 16th century BCE, and archeologists have found evidence of chariots before that date. Chariots were destined to dominate Chinese warfare for centuries. The other constant was invasion from northern nomads.

By 600 CE noble warlords driving their chariots into battle controlled Chinese warfare. Rituals were an important feature of warfare in this era. The aristocratic charioteers did not think of anything other than single duels with their chosen enemy, a noble of similar rank. One story tells of how two warriors exchanged bowfire. One fired an arrow and missed, but he was ready to shoot again before his opponent had fired. His opponent pointed out that this was unfair. The first warrior put down his bow and allowed his opponent to fire. The first warrior was killed.

Armies also did not engage in surprise attacks, ambushes, or even wage war on a state whose ruler had recently died. Usually armies exchanged messengers to arrange the time and place of battle. Before battle the ground would be smoothed over so that chariots

Sun Tzu, the author of *The Art of War*, one of the first military manuals. Sun Tzu proposed that generals should seek to win using strategy and intelligence, rather than by fighting.

SUN TZU'S *THE ART OF WAR*

In 1080 CE the Chinese emperor required all the officers of his army to be tested on their knowledge of the best military books. The oldest of these, and the oldest military manual in the world, was *The Art of War* by Sun Tzu. It is generally accepted that this short book was written during the sixth century CE. Sun Tzu, however, was not an original thinker. He collected together the standard military procedures of Chinese armies and presented them to his readers as an organized guide to the way a war should be fought. Nevertheless his book was an important manual.

Sun believed that war, and a battle in particular, were risky ways for a state to achieve its aims. He wrote that the best general was the one who won without fighting the bulk of his enemy's army. The way a general did this was to find the enemy's weak point and attack there. In the face of a stronger enemy Sun Tzu believed it was better to retreat.

would not have any trouble charging across it. Good manners were considered to be important.

Decline of Ritual

These military rituals became less important during the seventh century CE. Barbarians attacked China during the eighth century CE and destroyed the imperial capital, Hao, in 771 CE. The ruling dynasty, the Chou, had to move the imperial capital to Loyang.

The lord of Ch'in, a state in northwest China, fought off the barbarians, giving the emperor the protection he needed to get to Loyang. The emperor granted part of his lands to the lord of Ch'in. But this gesture reduced the power of the emperor.

By 500 CE there were three important states in China: Ch'in, north of the Yellow River, Ch'u, an area between the Yangtze and the Yellow Rivers, and Wu, controlling the coast between the mouth of the Yangtze and the Shantung Peninsula.

Between 519 and 506 CE Wu and Ch'u fought a major war that ended in Ch'u's destruction. To organize an army the king of Wu, He Lu, recruited many soldiers from his peasants, the first time any Chinese ruler had done this.

He Lu's peasant army marked the beginning of a major change in Chinese warfare. Peasant infantry replaced the aristocrats in their chariots as the most important troops. These foot soldiers were armed with crossbows or long spears. An era of constant conflict, known as the Warring States Period, began.

Seven main kingdoms were involved—Wei, Ch'i, Ch'u, Yen, Ch'ao, Han, and Ch'in. Wei was the strongest of the kingdoms but suffered major defeats in the middle of the fourth century CE at Ma Ling (353 CE) and Guai Ling (341 CE). These battles show that the old rituals of war were no longer used. In both cases the Wei forces were ambushed by their enemies.

Wei's defeats allowed two other states to expand. Ch'u advanced along the Yangtze River to the coast. Ch'in similarly gained greater control over the Yellow River. Between 315 and 223 CE these two states began a long conflict to settle the question of which of the two would dominate China.

In the wars of this time infantry was much the most important part of any army. Most infantrymen wore armor, but the best troops were lightly equipped. These were used to attack the flanks of an enemy army or were placed in reserve to race quickly into battle. While generals in European and Middle Eastern wars often fought in the front rank, Chinese generals remained behind the lines in a place where they could watch the battle in safety.

From their position in the rear they signaled to their troops by means of drums or gongs. A drumbeat told an army to advance, while beating a gong was the signal for withdrawal. Flags were also used to signal in which direction to move. To wave a flag to the right or left meant to move in those directions.

Cavalry with Bows

During the Warring States Period chariots remained the most important mounted arm, but cavalry also began to appear. Unlike the armies of Greece or Persia, where cavalry charged the enemy, the Chinese preferred the methods used by the nomads of the plains north of the Yellow River. These horse soldiers carried bows. They charged the enemy, firing arrows, then ride away. Only when their archery had caused enough casualties to frighten or

THE CH'IN MILITARY MACHINE

In 1974 archeologists digging in Sian in west-central China discovered the tomb of the Ch'in emperor Shih Huang Ti. Inside it was an entire life-size army made out of terra-cotta, presumably based on the soldiers of the emperor.

Unlike their counterparts in Europe and the Middle East, the Chinese gathered together archers and soldiers armed with spears in the same unit. The terra-cotta warriors did not carry shields but wore armor made up of small bronze plates sewn onto quilted jackets.

The Ch'in army also had much better cavalry than most Chinese armies. Some may have been equipped with crossbows. The bow was the preferred cavalry weapon, although the "cavalry" of the terra-cotta army had spears.

The emperor filled the ranks of his army from the small farmers of his realm. Any man between the ages of 17 and 60 owed service either as a soldier or as a laborer. The soldiers received pay and were fed from stocks of rice kept in fortresses across the empire.

Chinese mounted soldiers from the Qi period. Cavalry had become an important element in warfare in China during the Warring States Period.

weaken the enemy did they begin to fight hand-to-hand.

The Rise of Ch'in

By the middle of the third century CE Ch'in had become the dominant power in China. In 249 CE its king overthrew the Chou emperor, whom the Chinese states regarded as their supreme ruler, although he had no real authority. In 247 CE Ying Cheng, aged just 13, became king of Ch'in. In 228 CE he launched a war to conquer China and took the name Shih Huang Ti, "First Autocratic Emperor."

In 214 CE Shih Huang Ti colonized the area around Canton, the first time Chinese rule had reached so far south. He also began the construction of earth fortifications along the empire's northern border. His successors would replace these with the stone wall known today as the Great Wall of China. When Shih Huang Ti died, his generals began fighting a civil war to see which of them would inherit this great empire. In 207 CE there were only two main contestants left, Hsiang Yu and Liu Pang. Liu Pang triumphed at the Battle of Kai-hia in 202 CE. Liu Pang was the founder of the Han dynasty.

Glossary

armor A protective covering of the body made from cured animal hide, cloth, or metal.

barbarian A term applied by many of the ancient Mediterranean world's "civilized" states to any group who had not adopted their ways or language.

cavalry Soldiers mounted on horses, usually equipped with all or a combination of bow, sword, shield, and lance. Some cavalrymen wore armor, while others were lightly equipped to move fast.

chariot A two-wheeled war cart pulled by two or more horses. One of the crew controlled the chariot, while the other(s) carried bows and spears.

hoplite Heavy infantry troops, chiefly found in Greece. They wore armor and carried a large shield. Their chief weapons were a sword and spear. Hoplites fought in blocks many ranks deep.

horse-archers Mounted troops whose chief weapon was the bow. They were rarely armored and used their speed to avoid an enemy force.

legion Created by the Romans, legions had around 5,000 troops—legionaries. Their weapons were the shield, sword, and throwing javelin.

light infantry Soldiers who wore no heavy armor so as to improve their mobility. They were armed with missile weapons—the sling, bow, or javelin.

limes The lines of fortifications that protected the boundaries of the Roman Empire.

mercenary A soldier who fights for money or loot rather than for a belief or cause, and is not a citizen or subject of the country or state for which he is fighting.

peltast A type of light infantryman equipped with a sling, bow, or javelin.

phalanx A dense block of spearmen developed by the Greeks and copied by other ancient states.

trireme A wooden warship powered by sails and three banks of oars.

Further Reading

Cheriton Children's Books. *The Romans: Gory Gladiators and Cruel Conquerors.* Lerner Publications, 2023.

Kiley, Kenneth F. *An Illustrated Encyclopedia of Uniforms of the Ancient Greek World: A Detailed Study of the Fighting Men of Classical Greece and the Ancient World.* Lorenz Books, 2024.

Santillian, Beatriz. *Hadrian: Leaders of the Ancient World.* Rosen Publishing, 2018.

Santillian, Beatriz. *Ramses II: Leaders of the Ancient World.* Rosen Publishing, 2018.

Websites

education.nationalgeographic.org/resource/ancient-civilization-conquest/ National Geographic articles on different aspects of warfare in the ancient world.

online.kidsdiscover.com/quickread/triremes-triple-decker-warships-that-ruled-the-ancient-seas A short look at how Greek triremes were built and used in naval warfare.

pbs.org/empires/romans/empire/soldiers.html A Brief description of the Roman army at its most powerful.

Index